Sakagwa Ng'iti

A Kisii Prophet

Peter Nyambasora Okari

Copyright © 2021 Peter Nyambasora Okari
All rights reserved

This publication may not be reproduced, in whole or in part, by any means including photocopying or any information storage or retrieval system, without the specific and prior written permission of the author and publisher.

This book is sold subject to the condition that it shall not, by way of trade or otherwise, be re-sold, hired out, or otherwise circulated without the author's or publisher's prior consent in any form of binding or cover other than that in which it is published and without a similar condition including this condition being imposed on the subsequent purchaser.

First Edition (translation): June 2021

Published by Nsemia Inc. Publishers (www.nsemia.com); Oakville, Otario, Canada

Cover Concept & Illustration: Author
Cover Picture Credit: Sakagwa's Family
Cover Design: Linda Kiboma
Layout: Bethsheba Nyabuto
Project Consultant: Matunda Nyanchama

Note for Librarians:
A cataloguing record for this book is available from the Kenya National Library

ISBN: 978-1-989928-10-3

Dedication

To my dear mother, Omong'ina Marcella Kwamboka Okari

Acknowledgements

This book has come into reality through the support of many people who became sources of the material, provided ideas on its presentation and encouraged me to go the full length of ensuring its publication.

I owe a tremendous debt of gratitude to my mother who told me the story of Sakagwa several times as I grew up. This is one of the many stories my mother knew about people, places and Gusii culture which she shared with me in the course of our constant interaction. She was my first teacher on the values of prudence and hard work, much of which was embedded in the stories she told. With that she inspired me from a tender age and taught me to value the community folklore and our cultural grounding.

Of the many stories she recounted to me, that of Sakagwa stood out because of the influence and impact he had on the people of Gusii.

I acknowledge the wonderful support that my wife and the entire family offered me during the time of writing this book. Their patience with me and the accompanying encouragement fuelled my spirit to complete the project of writing this work.

A number of people offered background and finer details that helped refine this work to what it is now. They include the late Mzee Manoti Bw'Onsomu, Mr. Patrick Nyariki, Mr. Francis Gichana, Mr. Dismas Ateka and many others who freely shared information with me that enabled me to tie up this story together. Living family members of the family of Sakagwa kindly offered further information that up till now was not common knowledge. The information, offered generously, reinforced the value of the story told herein.

Without them, this work would be a scant version of what is presented here.

Dr. Andrew Rasugu Riechi read through the first draft of the book and offered critical input that enabled me to finalize the project. He also wrote the foreword for this work. I am truly grateful for both his efforts and feedback.

The team at Nsemia Inc. Publishers, led by Matunda Nyanchama, offered useful suggestions that ensured the story was properly laid out to communicate what was intended.

Finally, I thank my colleagues in St. Angela's School, especially Mwalimu Aloys Vincent, for typing the entire manuscript.

Peter Nyambasora, HSC
Kisii, Kenya
January 2021

Foreword

Among Abagusii, there are few precolonial historical figures that match the stature and awe of Sakagwa Ng'iti. A man who was much admired for his contribution to the community, and equally feared for his mysterious powers, Sakagwa stands tall like no other personality of his times and beyond.

He warned about the society's improprieties, deviation from acceptable norms and consequences thereof. Indeed, many attribute the calamity of the hunger of *enyamakongiro*, which happened following a prolonged drought in the 1800, to the failure of the community to heed his warnings. In this respect, he was the 'John the Baptist' of Abagusii.

His expertise and experience in the treatment of various body ailments using traditional medicine, an art inherited from his father, made him famous beyond the Gusii community.

Being different, Sakagwa faced suspicions from some in the community. In fact, the brutal murder of his first wife is attributed to such hostilities.

Having watched the constant defeat of Abagusii people in the hands of hostile ethnic groups such as the Maasai and the Kipsigis, Sakagwa was instrumental in the development of effective war strategies to forestall further defeats. Taking advantage of *ebisarate* and working with elders, they were able to train young men in the art of protecting the people and livestock. In the end, he helped forge rare unity among the different clans of Omogusii through oathing (*koria emuma*) that ensured that all people in the community united against external attacks. For the first time, Abagusii defeated the Kipsigis, courtesy of this unity! The war, famously known as Osaosao (battle of Sao Sao), became the last major conflict between the two ethnic groups.

Sakagwa prophesied the coming of the white person who would use the power of the 'smoking pipe', the gun. To this he asked Abagusii not to resist and assured them that the foreigners will eventually leave. As a result of the community not heeding his advice, Abagusii incurred many losses – in warriors' lives, properties and livestock.

The death of the sage remains a mystery, to date, for many.

A man of unusual gifts – rare insights, medicine-man, prophet and strategist – Sakagwa left an indelible mark on the trajectory of Abagusii as a people.

Sakagwa's story has been told in a number of flavours, many of them 'affirming' the mysterious life the sage lived. Clearly, few of these stories can match what Mwalimu Peter Nyambasora Okari has intelligently documented in this insightful book.

Mwalimu has weaved a credible account of Sakagwa's informed by many interviews, oral tales passed down through generations and (yes) some family secrets. With this approach, Mwalimu not only sheds fresh light into the story of the sage but also proffers explanations of many things that have remained mysterious to date. Indeed, finally, the matter of a grave without a body can be explained. The issue of the failure of succession of the sage's art of medicine and foretelling can be explained. And much more!

These new insights further inform the story of the sage and cement his place in the history of Abagusii, as well as the role of unique personalities like him in the survival of communities.

Finally, the story told herein challenges our generation to do more to preserve our history and heritage. Sakagwa's grave, the place where he held court and those he visited as he went about his work are community heritage sites. In this rare piece of work, Mwalimu affirms the place of history, heritage and community lore as part of our continuity into the future. Indirectly, he challenges us to preserve these for posterity.

As an epitome of lifelong learning, Mwalimu also challenges us all to write those stories that we come across or know but, perhaps, which we do not attach a lot of value to. We owe it to future generations to record these *untold stories* during our times on this earth.

Andrew Rasugu Riechi, PhD
Senior Lecturer in Economics of Education,
University of Nairobi.

Table of Contents

Dedication iii
Acknowledgements v
Foreword vii
Introduction xiii

Background **1**
  The Hostile World Sakagwa was Born Into 1
  Spiritual Belief & Worship 2
  The Path to Adulthood 4
  Ebisarate & Gusii Defence 7
  Sakagwa's Youth & Ebisarate 11

Sakagwa's Life and Ancestry **15**
  Ng'iti: Sakagwa's Father 15
  The Birth of an only Son 17
  Sakagwa's Early Life 19
  Young Man Sakagwa & Warring 23
  Adulthood and Back to Getwanyansi 24
  Sakagwa & First Wife Kerubo 27
  The Death of Kerubo 28
  Sakagwa's Second Wife – Kwamboka 31

Sakagwa & the Omogusii Community **33**
  Sakagwa as a Medicine Man 33
  Sakagwa as Rainmaker and Diviner 39
  Sakagwa as a Community Sage 41

Sakagwa – the Prophet 42

Sakagwa the Strategist and the Battle of Osaosao 53

Sakagwa in Old Age & Death 65
At Gesoni near *Chisokoro*............................65

The Farewell Party...70

Controversial Death, Burial and Consternation 74

Why Sakagwa's Death and Burial Confounds Many...87

Aftermath of Sakagwa's Death 91
Mumboism 91

Sakagwaism 96

Sakagwa's Family after His Death 101

Sakagwa School & 'Shrine'......................115
Sakagwa's Shrine 115

Sakagwa School..116

Conclusion: Sakagwa's Legacy 127
Glossary of terms.....................................135
Bibliography 139

Introduction

This is the story of a man who was many things to many people. As much as he is seen by some as a perfect person, he had many imperfections like most human beings. Over time, he developed a serious mission and vision in life. It was a prelude for him to become a great historical personality in Gusii, the land of Abagusii.

Sakagwa's[1] name, his movements, prophecies and treatment of ailments were well known throughout Gusii in his time. Indeed, at the start of the twentieth century, literary everyone in Gusii knew of Sakagwa and needed not be reminded of the great impact he left on the people of Gusii. Some of those reverberate to date.

More than a century on, the man's name surfaces continually and hardly anyone can speak of the story of Abagusii without the mention of Sakagwa. He is revered as a prophet, a medicine man, community leader and war strategist.

Unfortunately, not much has been written about him, especially in exploring the facts about his life, his family lineage, where he was born, how he grew up and the accomplishments of his lifetime.

It is our view that Sakagwa was a sage and philosopher in Gusii of the kind like Socrates, Plato, Mahatma Ghandi and others were. Informally, others liken him to prophet Jeremiah of the Old Testament. In the bible, Jeremiah's message to his people was, at all times, that of repentance

---

1Note that we have used the name 'Sakagwa' rather than 'Sakawa' as some people spell it. This is becacause we believe that the former is the correct spelling of the name based on the langauage of Ekegusii.

and salvation, rather than condemnation; it was a message that was full of richness of positive elements in traditional and ethnic culture. He was a prophet who preached what he lived by and what he believed in as did Sakagwa.

Sakagwa occupies a central role in the history of Abagusii, specifically his life and role in shaping the destiny of Omogusii. This book captures biographical information about Sakagwa, the son of Ng'iti and Nyabosungire, most of it passed down generations through oral tales and confirmed by interviews with the seer's descendants, among others. All efforts have been made to present the information in its original form. There is a chance that some of the information has been distorted and varied in interpretation due to passage of time.

In developing and presenting this work, efforts have been made to capture today's relevance of Sakagwa's pronouncements. We believe that, watching things unfold as they are doing today, affirms the seer's prophecies. This work is original and authentic. Most of it has been birthed, as it were.

I hope that the work presented here will inform and enrich the history, heritage and culture of Omogusii. It is also a challenge to others to address the yawning gaps in the history, culture and other aspects of Omogusii. Go ye forth and illuminate the depths of this knowledge and make it part of the global heritage.

Peter Nyambasora, HSC,
Kisii, Kenya
June 2021

Background

The Hostile World Sakagwa was Born Into

In the 1830s, the period within which Sakagwa was born, Abagusii must have been a small number of people, perhaps not more than 10,000 in total. They lived in a vast forested area and grew food crops such as finger millet (*obori*) which was the staple for the community. They kept livestock for milk and meat. Livestock was also the currency of the day. For example, when one was ready to marry, one paid the requisite dowry in a number of heads of cattle.

Hunting complemented their food sources. Here Abagusii hunted wild animals such as deer, elephants, gazelles and the like.

It was also the period after Abagusii had faced many tribulations. They had been routed out of Kabianga by the Kipsigis and had lost a major war against the Siria Maasai. In the latter, their leader Ongarora was felled in Trans Mara.

Weakened and dejected, Abagusii were constantly harassed by cattle raiders from the two ethnic groups. Such raids not only led to loss of livestock, they also left devastation in their wake. A raiding troupe could kill any men on their way, torch homes of the victims and take off with livestock and women.

There was more. According to W. R. Ochieng' in his book titled, *A Pre-Colonial History of the Gusii of Western Kenya. 1500–1914*, Abagusii faced an existential crisis. By the time Sakagwa was born, they had lost their lands in Kericho, Bomet and Trans Mara areas. The territories of the community were continuously shrinking in response to the expanding frontiers of their aggressive neighbours. Ochieng' writes that, by 1880, no Gusii families lived to the South of River Kuja due to the activities of the Kipsigis and the Maasai.

As if that was not enough, Abagusii community was threatened further with the potential of assimilation. John Akama, in his book *The Gusii of Kenya: Social, Economic, Cultural, Political & Judicial Perspectives* indicates that the numbers of Abagusii declined substantially at and around Kabianga. They faced a triple assault on their population: death from disease and famine, death from war; and assimilation of some of their own into the Kipsigis community. The latter, it is said, did so tactfully to assure their survival.

As well, according to William Ochieng', by the 1880s, 'most of the present-day Muksero and Wanjare people bordering with the Luo were also undergoing intensive acculturation'. This phenomenon was in part halted with the coming of the colonial administration.

Spiritual Belief & Worship

Abagusii of the time believed in the existence of one God, named *Engoro*, the Supreme Being, who was associated with the sun. Abagusii believed that *Engoro* created the universe, the earth and all the forces operating in it. In addition, *Engoro* was the original proprietor and source of property and life. As well, *Engoro* governed the destiny of man, sending him rain or storm, harvest or famine, health or disease, peace or war.

There was something about *Engoro* and the sun. Abagusii believed, and rightly so, that all life emanated from *Engoro* through the sun. When a child was born, a mother would pray for *Engoro*'s blessings in raising the child. Typically, she would make the child face the sun and utter the words *rioba nderera* (sun, raise my child for me).

Death, to Abagusii, was not the end of life. They believed that, on death, a person transformed into the spiritual world to live with the other ancestors, *chisokoro*. They also believed that these *chisokoro* had a continual effect on the living. If they were happy, the living would remain unperturbed. However, whenever *chisokoro* were unhappy, it could spell chaos for the culprits among the living. According to Abagusii, *chisokoro* also interceded for the living to assure their message reached *Engoro*.

It is for this reason that Abagusii, from time to time, offered sacrifices in order to appease *chisokoro*. Sacrifices were associated with various occurences, for example, the case of failure to have a child, a string of deaths of one's newly born children, unexplained phenomena such as thunder strikes, prolonged droughts or appearance of an owl in one's homestead.

Sacrifices were also used for cleansing. A person that committed a crime (for example killing a person, stealing from one's own, entering an unacceptable amorous liaison, etc.) would need to undergo an elaborate cleansing ceremony in order to be rehabilitated.

There is more. Medicine men (*abanyamete*; sing. *omonyamete*), witches and wizards (*abarogi*; sing.

omorogi), charm casters (*abanyamerisa*; sing. *omonyamesira*), exorcists (*abariori;* sing. *omoriori*), fortune tellers (*abaragori*; sing. *omoragori*), seers/prophets (*ababani*; sing. *omobani*) and others played a major role in that world.

Abanyamete (medicine men) treated ailments largely using herbs. They understood what herb had what effect on what ailment.

Abarogi were believed to have powers to bewitch people using intricate processes and items associated with their targets.

Abanyamesira could plant charms to harm individuals for one reason or the other.

Abariori were a unique group that practised exorcism. Typically, they could 'smell', locate and unearth charms secretly planted by either *abanyamesira* or *abarogi*. It is possible they played tricks on people's minds to convince them they had unearthed charms planted in compounds or houses of 'victims'.

The *abaragori* could unravel 'puzzles'; a typical *omoragori* would work with their paraphernalia to identify the cause of a specific problem or worry that their client presented. They would then do a diagnosis and offer a prescription such as undergoing cleansing or offering a sacrifice.

Ababani were the typical prophets that kept the community in check and warned of consequences that might come and hurt the community in future. Prophets typically provided the community with choices: repent and all will be well. Failure to repent, though, could bring wrath to the community or part of it.

It was often the case that the roles overlapped

and one person could play such multiple roles. For example, seers could also be medicine men as would be exorcists.

In Gusii of the time, all these roles had spiritual connotations and individuals who had the associated powers often went through elaborate proceses to of concecration to acquire them. Often, those who conducted such ceremonies, played a spiritual role themselves.

The Path to Adulthood

Boys and girls grew up following a specified path based on the four *chinyangi* (rites of passage) for everyone in the community, which were: birth, initiation to adulthood, marriage and death.

Gender roles were also well-defined with boys and girls following the tutelage path for men and women, respectively. For the latter, mothers, grandmothers and aunts were crucial in shaping the characters and lives of women.

For boys, the process was similar where older boys and men acted as mentors, trainers and guardians of young boys.

It was typical for boys to join older men in encampments called *ebisarate (*sing. *egesasate).* According to Prof. John Akama[1], the concept of *ebisarate* evolved as a necessary defense strategy against enemy cattle raiders. *Ebisarate* were also

---

1 **Editor's Note:** in *The Untold Story of the Gusii of Kenya: Survival Techniques and Resistance to the Establishment of British Colonial Rule* (Nsemia Inc., 2019), John Akama says that *ebisarate* can be seen as military encampments where you boys were trained to be warriors and imbued with military-style discipline necessary for the protection of the community.

used as units of defence or hideouts. Members of the community could take refuge there when it was necessary. Cattle, the currency of wealth of the time, needed special protection as any loss meant loss of wealth to the community. Indeed, the incessant wars with ethnic groups like the Maasai and Kipsigis were about cattle. In this regard, *ebisarate* served as units or bases where warriors trained and stayed; ready to defend against attacks or raids from outside.

Further, *gesarate* thus became a special area where men and young adults stayed when they excluded themselves from the rest of their kinsmen for various purposes. It was here that boys became men in the true sense of the word.

Ebisarate were constructed in homesteads for the reasons enunciated above. A typical *egesarate* had residents (newly initiated young men under the guidance of older men), accommodated livestock and was built strategically to make it hard to penetrate by raiders. At *gesarate* young men, through incisive training, learnt to become warriors, and were trained on defense techniques and use of weapons such as spears, shields, bows and arrows as well as sling shots.

The young warriors were taught defence techniques such as how best they could attack an enemy and what they were expected to do when overwhelmed by the opponent.

In addition, young men were imparted with positive character traits, community responsibility and protecting the weak and vulnerable.

At *gesarate* the young men learnt from their seniors that they were no longer children but men who would be relied upon during happy and sad times, in times of peace and war. At *gesarate*, as the warriors underwent rigorous training, they were given a number of strict rules. Through this training, the warriors would devote themselves wholeheartedly to the defence of the community, believing that through the skills attained from the training, life and the wealth of the clan/tribe could be protected and maintained. At the *ebisarate* the training included many activities that also contributed to bonding such as wrestling and mock fighting! They also included the use of various weapons and associated war strategies. Warriors could use *bhang* liberally as a pastime.

Egesarate(Eburi)

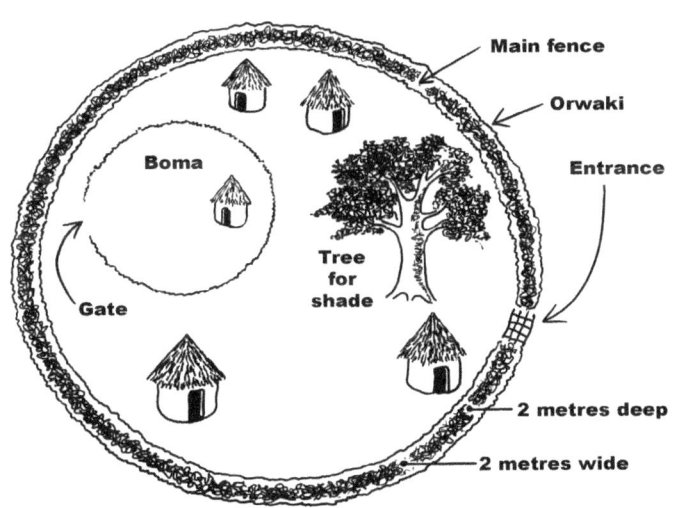

Ebisarate & Gusii Defence

Like any ideas and artefacts, the concept of *gesarate* and its utility evolved over time. Initially, *gesarate* (the place) meant a shade or hut in a homestead where the homestead head would invite and meet friendly elders for the exchange of news and ideas. The original name for *egesarate* was *eburi*.

Over time, *gesarate* became a typical isolated compound that was built some distance away from the homestead for purposes of protection of livestock from being stolen by raiders. It was constructed at some convenient site where the cows and other livestock could be kept especially in the night in a secure environment.

With time, *ebisarate* evolved to become encampments in which the entire livestock of a village or sub clan was kept during the night. In this respect, *ebisarate* were used as 'bomas' where cattle were always brought together to stay for the night after being counted by the warriors to be sure that none had been lost. It was presumed that *ebisarate* were the safest havens where the animals could have maximum protection in case of attack by raiders. Typically, *ebisarate* were built on a clan basis and each clan had its own *egesarate*.

Remember that, at the time, Abagusii were essentially dependent on cattle for their livelihood, and hence the idea of communal protection of their cattle was paramount. This is because individual Gusii homesteads found it extremely difficult to protect their livestock from well-armed raiders, who sometimes came in large numbers. *Gesarate* harnessed the communal spirit and leveraged numbers in which everyone participated; this process pooled efforts towards the collective protection of their livestock. As such, everybody who owned cattle would send a son, or sons, to stay with other young men from other homesteads to ensure that the livestock was safe.

In this respect, *ebisarate* were necessitated by the need for security at the time. Indeed, the numerous and constant raids from the Maasai and Kipsigis warriors contributed to their evolution in this direction.

We suspect that *ebisarate* became commonplace soon after Abagusii settled in the Gusii highlands at the beginning of the nineteenth century. This was long before the coming of the white men, and even before the birth of Sakagwa.

Inside one *egesarate*, there were about five or six huts. The huts were surrounded by two fences at a distance of about thirty metres from the centre of the compound. The main fence was built inside and the secondary fence (*orwaki*) outside. In between two fences, there was a trench, about two meters wide and two metres deep. The trench itself had spikes or sharp protruding objects at the bottom. The trench was meticulously covered to conceal its presence. Woe unto one who fell into the trench! They might never come out alive!

If or when one of the *egesarate* was attacked by enemies, usually raiders from another tribe, members in the other *ebisarate* in the neighbourhood would join forces to confront the common enemy. When the enemy was driven back, he could expect further attacks from any *egesarate* when the youthful warriors would be lying in wait along the path of retreat.

The young men or warriors who lived in the *ebisarate* were normally armed and would keep watch in turns, at night. Their leaders would usually be chosen from the most senior and toughest warriors. Aside from assuring order at *ebisarate*, the leaders would take part in giving instructions in preparation for battle and at the battlefront.

Typically, those who were married did not stay in *gesarate*. If one was married and stayed there, he was not allowed to be visited by his wife at the place. Indeed, women were not allowed in *gesarate*, except for the purpose of bringing food and when there was the need to hide from an attacking enemy. Nevertheless there was always sufficient food in *gesarate* – milk, roast meat from wild animals, blood bled from domesticated animals and wild fruits.

Life in *gesarate* followed an unwritten, yet understood, code. Elders always kept tabs on what was happening. As such, any warriors going against established code could face consequences: appropriate punishment administered by the elders.

The lead warrior of any clan was always a well-known and respected within the clan. He would be the man in charge of all clan warriors whose ages normally ranged from eighteen to forty years. These warriors were well grounded in the art of warfare. They knew how to handle various weapons like spears, clubs, arrows and shields.

At that time, people used traditional methods of communication to raise alerts about attacks, real and perceived. This included screaming, whistling, blowing a horn or beating a drum.

Whenever there was a call for attention, be it from a horn or drum, the warriors knew it as a signal that trouble was brewing and the reaction was instructive. The young men would immediately leave whatever they were doing and dash to 'armouries'. They would pick the necessary weapons and head in the general direction of trouble. The clan military leader would often be among the first warriors to arrive at the scene. He would lead his co-warriors to take their positions according to his command.

Note that clan warriors typically collaborated to thwart attacks when the perceived enemy forces appeared overwhelming. This happened despite the occasional squabbles amongst different clans.

Sakagwa's Youth & *Ebisarate*

As will be seen in the next section, Sakagwa, as a young man, grew up in an environment of constant siege from enemy tribes and at a time Abagusii had developed *ebisarate* as defensive/protective techniques. This was a time when clan identities of Omogusii were in formation and the various Gusii divisions were already established.

For example, for the Kitutu clan, this followed the peace which the various Kitutu clan elders (later to be called chiefs following colonialism) starting with Oisera, had imposed in the region. This was made possible by the use of small groups of armed warriors, recruited from all sub-clans of Kitutu who could be called upon by the clan heads to deal with weighty matters at hand, including insubordination. The reward for the warriors was land and cattle which various raiding parties collected from the Luo, the Kipsigis, the Maasai or other Gusii clans[2].

There were many *ebisarate* in Gusii, all of different sizes and strengths. Not even the

---

2 Yes, occasionally, clans raided each other, something that could result in inter-clan skirmishes.

Background

Abagusii elders knew all of them and they have yet to be formally documented. People would only know those in their locations or those associated with their clans; the ones that served their needs. For instance, somebody from Nyaribari or North Mugirango was not likely to know the ones in Kitutu.

*****

Sakagwa is said to have followed the path of other young men of his time. He joined the other warriors (call it the ethnic army) when he came of age. The army was made of young Gusii warriors and was a natural destination once a young man was initiated into adulthood. In this army, Sakagwa learnt war skills, techniques and tactics like his peers.

On joining other warriors, as was the case for young men of his time, Sakagwa stayed in *gesarate* for some years. As was the routine of the time, he and other warriors were subjected to rigorous training and a number of very strict rules that created order. Folklore has it that, while in there, he displayed admirable qualities of leadership. With time, he became better known for his discipline and wisdom and commanded great respect among his peers.

Soon, he had to leave the ethnic army to perform other activities. Before leaving *gesarate*, and having stayed there for some years and gained the necessary experience, he encouraged the young warriors, as well as the elders to preserve and strengthen the establishments and the defense mechanisms in the *ebisarate.* He believed that this was the only way they could defend the community against external enemies.

From *gesarate*, Sakagwa went back to the community, which was in bitter conflicts within itself and with external forces such as conflict with the Kipsigis and the Maasai. These were hard times of suffering for the community. In such times, communities yearned for people (prophets, counsellors) who could diagnose the causes of suffering, and provide foresight to pull them ou of the morass of troubles; people who could predict the future based on existing circumstances.

*****

We must understand that Sakagwa grew up and found the practices of *gesarate* in place. *Ebisarate* in Gusiil were in existence long before the birth of Sakagwa. Aside from going through the processing of living in *gesarate* like any boys of his time, he cannot be associated with their evolution.

That said, later in his life Sakagwa did build some huts that came to be known as *Ebigendi bia Sakagwa*. Sakagwa built these small huts at the far end of Kitutu location where nobody else was living, at the boundary of Bogetutu and Nyaribari. The area was densely forested and full of wild animals whose company Sakagwa seemed to enjoy in his solitude.

The dense forest was largely composed of trees called *emetembe* – hence the name *Getembe*, the original name of present-day Kisii Town.

It would later be known as *Getembe kia Gasuku*[3], after a man who was a court interpreter. Mr. Kasuku, a man from Suba, was translator for

---

3 'Gasuku' is a 'corruption' of the name 'Kasuku' which Abaugusii pronounced as such.

white colonial officers. He later became the interpreter at the Kisii Court that sentenced Otenyo Nyamaterere, the foremost Gusii warrior, to death. This, however, was long after Sakagwa's death.

Sakagwa's Life and Ancestry

Ng'iti: Sakagwa's Father

Sakagwa's father, Ng'iti, came from the Bogeka clan of Bogetutu and was known for his knowledge and skills as a medicine man and rainmaker.

It is not clear how and from whom he acquired these skills and knowledge. However, for Abagusii of the time, such roles as he held were passed down generations along family lines through extensive tutelage. It is possible that Ng'iti received the same from his father.

Ng'iti's lineage to Mogusii is shown in the diagram below. He was the son of Nyakembugumbugu, whose father was Ogeka (the father of Bogeka sub clan in Bogetutu). In turn, Ogeka was the son of Nyakundi who was the son of Oisera. Oisera's father was Tabichi the son of Mosweta Ngoge. On the other hand, Mosweta Ngoge was the son of Oibabe, the second born son of Mogusii (father of Abagusii).

The father of Abagusii, nicknamed Gwea Nyakebagancha, Mogusii had four (4) sons: Tereri (also known as Mobasi), Oibabe, Mochorwa and Motabori; he had one daughter, Monchari[1]. Mochorwa and Motabori were twins.

Mogusii was the son of Osogo (Onsongo in

---

1 (a) Some accounts have it that there was another daughter called Mokeira. However, the larger number of our references suggest that Mokeira could have been a grandchild rather than a daughter of Mogusii. Clearly, this is a case that calls for further research; (b) Monchari, the descendant of Abanchari is said to have been married in Luoland to a man called Machabe but later relocated with her children to Gusii.

Ekegusii) and Nyakomogendi. From oral tales, both parents of Mogusii are believed to have died at Kisumu, and were buried there.

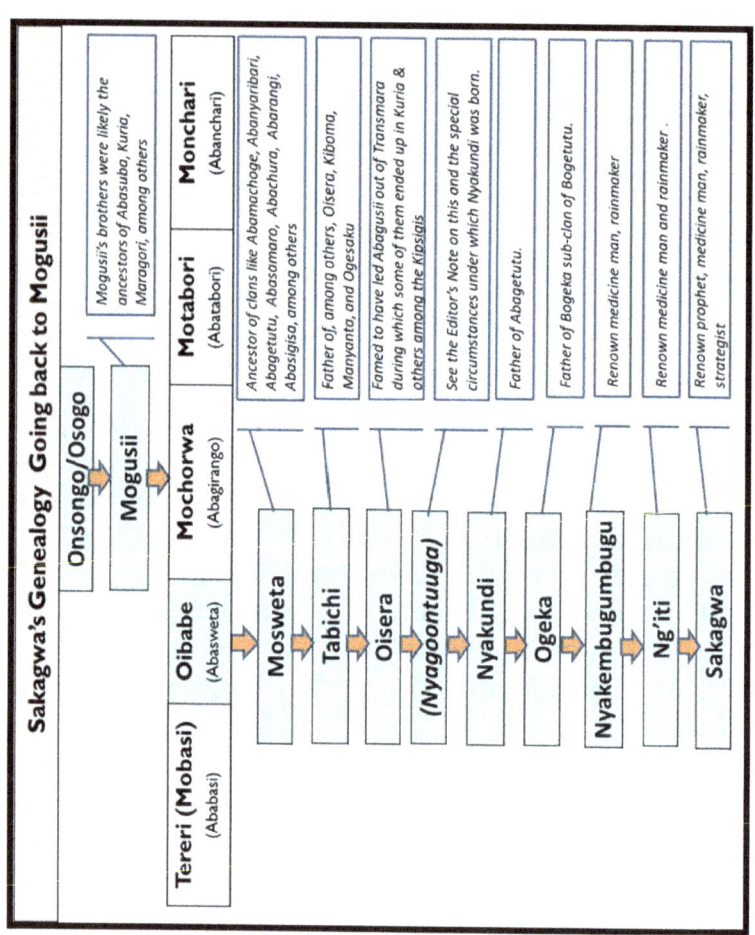

Editor's Note: *in the* Song of a Blacksmith and Totems of Abagusii, *Evans Getuma Mogaka traces the origins of Abagetutu to two women: Nyakomogori and Nyagoontuuga; the former, the eldest wife of Oisera had many daughters but no sons and she wished to have her lineage perpetuated but did not want anything to do with sons of her cowives.*

As such she organized a wedding where she impersonated the groom and brought home a bride who would sire grandchildren for her. The woman she brought home was Nyagoontuuga who sired a child (Nyakundi - father of Abagetutu) with a man who was from Bogusero sub-clan. As such, strictly speaking, Nyakundi was a grandchild of Oisera!

Ng'iti, was a powerful magician and medicine man. It is said that sometimes he could stay in the bush for several days, enjoying the company of wild animals like snakes, lions, leopards, and hyenas. It is claimed that he understood the language of these animals and could effectively communicate with them.

Similarly, Ng'iti had a wide knowledge of herbs, which made him a great herbalist and rainmaker, attributes that he would later bequeath his son Sakagwa.

The Birth of an only Son

Sakagwa was born at a place called Getwanyansi in the Manga area, in Bogetutu in present-day Kisii County. No records of his birth exist considering that, at the time, Abagusii passed information orally down generations. However, through deductions based on the events that took place during his early life, we estimate that he was born in the early 1830s. His parents were Ng'iti and Moraa Nyabosungire.

Sakagwa was born when his father, Ng'iti, was at an advanced age. Ng'iti had many wives, with whom he begot many daughters but, apparently, only one son, whom he named Sakagwa. Stories told over the ages hold that the old man desperately wanted a son to carry on his heritage as a medicine man and rainmaker in the community. For him, the birth of his son Sakagwa was *Engoro*'s[2] assurance that the art would be available for future generations.

Gusii society is patriarchal and inheritance is passed from father to son. This placed high premium on siring boys, and a man with no son would be seen as one with doomed lineage. Abagusii reasoned that since girls would get married away at some stage and leave the homestead, the boy would remain to perpetuate continuity of the family lineage and the patriarch's wealth, procreate to sire future generation and inherit that which was transmissible between generations, such as the healing and seer powers. Boys were also required to take care of their parents when the latter got into old age. Thus, once a boy was born, there were remarkable celebrations to welcome him to the family, unlike in the case of the birth of a girl.

A woman who did not sire a boy was typically looked down upon. She was seen as not being 'woman enough'. To continue the lineage, her alternative was to get a woman (call her a daughter in-law) and have the younger woman bear grandchildren for the older woman. These children would be borne with the help of a selected man, who would be a 'son' to the older woman in the family tree[3].

The case was not different for the man. He could be reduced to a laughing stock by peers, especially in social gatherings such as those where men congregated to partake of brew. However, since

2 Abagusii's name for God..
3 The case of Nyakundi the father of Abegetutu, as covered elsewhere in this book, illustrates this point.

society allowed men to marry more than one wife, such a man could marry again with the hope that the newly married wife would be lucky and give birth to a boy. In fact, in some cases, the first wife would be the one taking a lead in searching for a co-wife. Clearly, the society of the time did not appreciate that, in conception, it is the man that determines a child's gender.

As such a boy, once born, was jealously protected to assure his survival. At all costs, no family would want to lose a child, particularly a boy, for without a son, a man or woman's lineage was as good as gone.

Sakagwa's Early Life

Sakagwa as the only son received special attention from his family as the heir to Ng'iti's heritage. Specifically, his father bestowed all attention he could on the young boy. Ng'iti gave his son all the love, laced with a lot of hope for the future. It is said that he made the boy his apprentice at an early age. So pretty early in his life, Sakagwa learnt the art of rainmaking and the use of herbs for treating various ailments.

It is said that the youngster had a penchant for learning, for he showed eagerness to understand whatever came his way. As such, he keenly followed and emulated his father's actions at every turn as the older person went about his trade. Because of this practical training, Sakagwa not only learnt the names of the medicinal plants well, but he also mastered the plants' nutritional and medicinal value at a tender age.

In addition to this, he learnt the customs and rules of good behaviour towards members of society, including older people and peers. His closeness with his father enabled him to fully internalize legendary stories, riddles and proverbs of Abagusii passed down generations.

*****

The community of the time had no clothes of the kind we see today. Both men and women fashioned their attire from animal skins and plants. Women wore *chingobo* (sing. *engobo*) that covered the waist downwards. Men, on the other hand, wore *ebisena* (sing. *egesena*) that covered their backside (mainly the buttocks) and frontline (the manhood). Both *chingobo* and *ebisena* were fashioned from dried animal skins. Others would complement these attires with dried banana leave sheaths.

As with all others, Sakagwa went with the dressing of the time. He fashioned his clothing mainly from dried banana sheaths. It is said that he had a hairy body and very long hair that grew to cover even his ears.

*****

It is further said that, very early on, the young Sakagwa showed meditative tendencies. He could spend a lot of time in complete isolation, except when his father would take him along to the forest to look for herbs. Whenever he was left behind, the young Sakagwa would disappear into nearby bushes and sit all alone. Other times, while meditating, he could sit on a hill or by a river and lose himself in deep thought, oblivious of what was happening around him.

It is said that Sakagwa hardly talked to people, unless it was very necessary. In fact, many people thought that he had a speech impairment, dumb in other words.

It is possible that, by taking time out in solitude and to be with nature, Sakagwa allowed himself access to his deepest thoughts and possibly the human spirit with which we are all gifted. However, one has to experience this to believe it, according to those who believe in the benefits of meditation. It is a wonderful energizer, they aver. Even the Holy Book, the Bible, tells us that Jesus Himself sometimes took time out to be alone and meditate.

It is said that Sakagwa never bothered people around him nor was he bothered with what many of them did. He just loved to do what he loved: being alone, reflecting and meditating.

People with an 'abundance mentality' usually seek solitude and seem to enjoy the world around them. This a mentality based on one doing what one loves and the belief that 'there is enough to go around' and that 'you can still be rich with or without having material wherewithal'. Further, such a mentality allows for the exploration of possibilities that may not be obvious to others without a similar perspective.

People with this mentality take time out to enjoy nature's creation and appreciate the beauty of the universe. They marvel at how much God has provided in the beautiful diversity of creation.

Sakagwa's search for solitude and reflection at that early age we believe, was a demonstration of the abundance mentality. This is where and when one can observe how fulfilling a prophecy it is to believe that God has provided for us abundantly.

Indeed, it can be argued further that, it is such a mentality that enabled him, later in life, to see possibilities (like the unity of Gusii clans against foreign attackers) that allowed for results that hitherto were not perceived.

*****

Sakagwa grew up during a very troubled period in Gusii. As indicated in the Background section, the people of Gusii were under constant siege from aggressive neighbours. As well, they were not spared by famines and epidemics that were rampant and ravaged the land. Worse still, the community was fragmented along clan lines and hence could not act in unison to assure its survival. All these shaped Sakagwa's outlook and made him a product of that environment and time, as it were.

It is possible that his moments of solitude gave him a good perspective of the society of the time, the challenges it faced and the possible responses, if any, to these challenges.

By the time Mzee Ng'iti died, Sakagwa had already become accomplished in his father's trade and was practising rainmaking and treating diseases with herbs in his own right. Incidentally, Sakagwa's first patient was Mzee Ng'iti, his father.

Information passed down over the years is that, as Mzee Ng'iti advanced in age, his health kept deteriorating. The combinaton of age and disease took their toll and that, towards the old man's death, Sakagwa made frantic efforts to treat the ailment. Prior to the old man dying, and over a period of three days, Sakagwa tried to treat his father using all the best herbs that he had learnt but all was in vain. At the end of it, Mzee Ng'iti died in the hands of his son, Sakagwa!

Alone, he had to assume his father's role in the community and more.

Young Man Sakagwa & Warring

As was the routine of the time, Sakagwa joined other young men at *gesarate* when he came of age. This was a time of frequent wars in Gusii occasioned by raids by the Maasai and even more by the Kipsigis. Typical of the path taken by young men of his age, Sakagwa joined the fighting force of the community. Like his peers, he trained at *gesarate* and here was the opportunity to put to use those skills gained in defence of the community. Community lore has it that Sakagawa stood out as a good warrior in encounters his contingent faced.

At one time, the constant raids in North Mugirango by the Kipsigis called for reinforcements and Sakagwa was one of those picked for the assignment. It is reported that that specific war became protracted because the Kipsigis were joined by their cousins, the Nandi, and the whole region was plunged into military turmoil.

The Kipsigis (actually the Kalenjin in general) and the Maasai, as history has it, were attached to cattle. They strongly believed that all the cattle in the world belonged to them. As such, when they raided another ethnic group's *bomas*, they were simply 'taking their property' back, they believed.

This is what the war in North Mugirango was about: the raiding Kipsigis who wanted to take cattle belonging to Abagusii and Abagusii resisting the raids to keep their livestock.

In the said battle, Abagusii managed to triumph against the Kipsigis and the Nandi. This was in part because Abagusii had perfected the art of training warriors and developed techniques that allowed the warriors to subdue the enemy. For instance, for reasons of security, Abagusii had their homesteads surrounded by thick thorn fences along which deep trenches were built. The trenches were then filled with dangerous spikes that were cleverly concealed, and only the people of the homestead knew where the safe entrance was. An attacking force would target a *boma* and end up with most of its warriors in the trenches, pierced to death by the dangerous spikes.

*****

There is more. Sakagwa had a chance to show his prowess as a medicine man and leader. During training and in war situations, some warriors could be wounded. Here Sakagwa would be called upon to help, becoming very useful in applying the knowledge and skills gained from his father.

There was a process followed in administering the medicine. Typically, it would be accompanied with unsalted soup made of a goat or sheep. For the patients who did not respond quickly to this treatment, Sakagwa would kill a snake (only he knew which type of snake) and burn it. The ashes would then be mixed with water and be given to the wounded person to drink. It is said that this type of treatment was very effective and Sakagwa received high recognition because of this role in treating the injured and sick in the battlefield.

*****

After the battle in North Mugirango Sakagwa, came back to Getwanyansi. He was now a full grown adult.

Adulthood and Back to Getwanyansi

Sakagwa's return to his home coincided with many calamities in Gusii. As a result of recurrent droughts there were constant famines causing undue suffering to the people. The raids from neighbouring enemy communities did not help.

Soon Sakagwa settled down to practise his trade as a medicine man, a herbalist. His lessons on rainmaking from his father also came in handy. Soon, he became recognized as a great rainmaker. Over time, his other specialities started to show.

It soon became obvious to Abagusii that Sakagwa was in possession of some special attributes as a seer, a medicine man, a rainmaker and a magician all rolled into one.

He could foresee things and warn society against practices that could jeopardize their survival! Here, he could pronounce matters that could suggest insights into the future and caution the community against excesses in their conduct and in the process urge them be modest and humble.

Further, his prowess in successfully treating ailments became entrenched as he applied the full knowledge and skills gained from his father's tutelage!

There was more!

Sakagwa could successfully summon the community to stage *ribina* (sing; plural: *amabina*) - the rain dance – when there were droughts. Reportedly, soon after the dance, followed by his rituals, it would fall in torrents!

In general, all these qualities elevated Sakagwa's

stature in Gusii. Moreover, these attributes and the various powers which he possessed meant that his services were sought across Gusii. Soon, even the 'enemies' of Abagusii – namely the Luo, the Maasai and the Kipsigis – started seeking him out.

Aside from offering his services, the interactions, especially with the Luo, Kipsigis and the Maasai enabled him to have useful insights about the thinking of the needs of their peers and these neighbours of Abagusii.

All this meant that many people (especially Abagusii clan elders) could come to him for counsel. The inside knowledge gained from interacting with 'enemies' no doubt came in handy when he was called upon to advise Abagusii on what preparation was required and what course of action to take in case of conflicts.

It was therefore small wonder that Sakagwa's assurances often gave Abagusii renewed energy and confidence when going into battle, or in any of the undertakings over which they sought his advice. For example, whenever there was drought or pestilence in Gusii, people would flock to him for help.

Sakagwa dispensed his services for free and this earned him the love of his people and even foreigners. This was in line with the beliefs of the time that such powers came from the yonder, and they were meant for the good of humanity. As such any misuse, for example through profiting, could lead one to lose those powers.

For Sakagwa, dispensing treatment was a ritual. Before dispensing medicines, and as was the tradition, he always consulted ancestral spirits, *chisokoro*. Like the common knowledge of the time, Sakagwa believed that *Engoro*, working through *chisokoro,* was the source of his strength and powers, so to speak.

As time passed, Sakagwa's position, given his rare gifts, became entrenched. He dispensed medicines and treated diseases. He was a rainmaker, had rare comprehension of matters of the community, and had insights into warring that few had. Most importantly, Sakagwa had an unusual ability of foreseeing many things of the future; he was developing into a prophet in the community.

Sakagwa & First Wife Kerubo

Back at Getwanyansi in Mwamosioma sub clan Sakagwa had matured and needed to do what all mature men did at the time – get married and start a family. Following the tradition of the time, he married his first wife Kerubo. They sired two sons and two daughters, namely, Riogi, Nyamacharara, Obare and Kemunto.

As covered elsewhere in this work, even as he worked to bring up the family, Sakagwa continued to dispense medicine, act as counsel for many and offer predictions. These capabilities made him different and not everyone was happy with him. Indeed, this was the case whenever his predictions became true. Sensing hostility, Sakagwa relocated to Sengera.

His reputation 'followed' him to his new home and he never found happiness either at Sengera as some people conspired to eliminate him. It is said that he predicted the attack and escaped. Meanwhile, his adversaries ended up as fodder for lions, something they attributed to the seer's powers.

His next station was Kiong'anyo where he did not stay for long and had to relocate to Kanyimbo in search of safety.

The Death of Kerubo

The story is told that when Sakagwa migrated from Kiong'anyo to settle in Kanyimbo with his family, strange incidents began to happen in the place. Such occurrences included unexplainable deaths of some people, especially young children. Others were cases of some people having mental issues (call it 'madness') and even others becoming deaf while others became dumb, completely losing the power of speech.

The community at Kanyimbo blamed Sakagwa's wife[4] for the strange happenings. Some people started spreading stories, mostly unfounded and unproven, that Sakagwa's wife was a night runner, a witch. However, they feared to report her to Sakagwa because they knew he would likely do nothing about it, though he was a medicine man himself. They believed that Sakagwa was aware of all this! Whether Sakagwa's wife was a night

---

4 **Editor's Note:** in Ekegusii, it is said that *'tiyana gokwa etaberegeti getondo'*, nothing happens without reason. Hence, based on the beliefs of the time, no one died without cause, 'being killed'. And since disease was poorly understood, deaths could be attributed to envy and caused by witchcraft. It is possible that the people of Kanyimbo associated these strange things to the new comers, the family of Sakagwa. And it was often the case that witchcraft was associated with women.

runner or not, is a question nobody could answer or prove at the time.

*****

Strange as this may sound, in many societies in Africa, especially during Sakagwa's time, there were beliefs that night runners, witches and wizards, existed and that they were up to no good. As such, the existence of night runner terrorizers was absolutely unquestioned! In fact, it happens to date in some parts of Gusii. At the time, there were stories told about the harm that could be unleashed by these 'evil rogues and masters' of the dark nights.

One of such harms that was believed to be possible was the silence spell cast on a villain which could reduce the victim to a speechless state and utter dumb struck! The victim could totally become gaga!

Possibly, because of the popular and unfounded belief that the night-runners could actually cause evil on whoever chanced upon them, many of the victims in the end succumbed to unexplainable deaths. On the other hand, some individuals were said to succumb to premature death after coming face to face with a night-runner or after ascertaining that his or her nocturnal tricks are aimed at him or at his entire household.

The mere feeling that the night-runner had made one's home the object of pranks rather than another home can be psychologically tormenting which can give rise to a fixation or some form of phobia that traumatizes the ego to death. It is possible that some people ended up affected, even died, since the disturbed vagal system can produce immediate adverse effects that can leave a person paralyzed or dumb permanently or for a period of time. It is small wonder that popular accounts have it that victims of personal encounters with the night-runners immediately lose the capacity for speech. We speculate that this is due to overwhelming fear that is caused following such an encounter. Once the fear inhabits the normal functioning of the principal cranial nerves, we suspect that it results in an inexplicable paralysis or loss of memory and speech.

Even so, another school of thought avers that the whole idea of witchcraft is mysterious and beyond human beings' ability to fathom and explain.

*****

It was in such a scenario that Sakagwa's wife was killed. Stories passed down generations indicate that she was ambushed one night, supposedly when she was on her nocturnal activities and strangled to death. Her body, the tales hold, was dumped in-front of her house.

This was a tragic moment for the Sakagwa family, especially the children. To find their mother brutally killed and the body dumped at their door step must have been a shock of their lives.

As the custom was at that time, burial was carried out immediately a person died. So, Sakagwa and his children organized and buried his wife without much ado.

Sakagwa's Second Wife – Kwamboka

Following the death of his first wife at Kanyimbo, Sakagwa married a second wife by the name Kwamboka whose maiden name was Getonto.

They would later be blessed with three children, namely, Nyamweno, Kemuma and Mogire.

The family stayed at Kanyimbo until such a time that the children were grown up. Later Sakagwa would move his entire family to Gesoni[5] in Bogeka, between Nyakoe and Mosocho.

Although it was normal at that time for people to move from one area to another, Sakagwa's migration from Kanyimbo to Bogeka was perhaps due to the bad memories the family had relating to the murder of his first wife by the community in Kanyimbo.

Other factors could also have contributed to his decision. By this time Sakagwa was advancing in age. It is possible that he wanted to settle down at a place close to his ancestors in his ancestral clan.

Further, at the time of relocation, there was a biting famine ravaging the land. It is possible that the family relocated to be close to his people where he could be assured of support; support that he could possibly not get from the unfriendly people of Kanyimbo.

---

5 The place now called Gesoni was originally known as Getare. In Ekegusii, *egetare* is a rock and hence *Getare,* a rocky place! The name Gesoni has its origin in the rainmaking dances that were held in the place. *Gosona* in Ekegusii means to 'admire', 'drool' or 'be sensually provoked'. It is possible that the rain dances were sensually provocative and hence the name.

Sakagwa & the Omogusii Community

Sakagwa played many roles among Abagusii which have been alluded to in the previous sections. In this chapter we outline some of those distinct roles. However, we note that these roles overlapped and the analysis done here is based on our perspective for the sake of clarity and understanding.

Sakagwa as a Medicine Man

Ng'iti, having been blessed with an only son, focused his entire attention in raising the boy, Sakagwa. He set out to ensure that Sakagwa would inherit his skill and knowledge and carry forward the family heritage in service of future generations. Ng'iti himself likely acquired the art from his father Nyakembugumbugu.

As such, from a very early age Sakagwa learnt many ideas and skills through his apprenticeship with his father. Just before Ng'iti died, he bestowed not only his love on his only son, but all his healing powers and knowledge. It is said that, as was the tradition, Ng'iti blessed his son and handed over to him all powers and accompanying paraphernalia from ancient times. The act may be likened to those from Biblical times where a parent blesses a favourite child. The case of Esau and Jacob in the bible is a good example.

As a young herbalist, Sakagwa, like his father, loved and enjoyed the company of wild animals. Some believed that he could communicate with the animals, just as it was with his father. As was the tradition of the time, people who held such unique positions in society believed that they were appointed by *Engoro*, through intercession of *chisokoro*, to serve the community. As such, Sakagwa also believed that *chisokoro* sought him out to articulate their wishes to Abagusii, particularly when the living erred.

It is possible that his belief that he was 'chosen' for the purpose eventually led him to the realization that conventional customs and beliefs were no longer the cementing factors of the Gusii community.

*****

From tales passed down generations, Mzee Ng'iti was Sakagwa's first patient! It is said that the last days of the old man were very tormenting due to sickness that confined him to his 'bed'. His only son would sit at the bedside trying to comfort the father and even asking which herbs or in which way he could help to alleviate the pain caused by the illness. Ng'iti would send Sakagwa to the forest to bring specified herbs and prepare them for drinking with the hope of getting better. Unfortunately, Sakagwa would spend a whole day looking for the herbs and, on many occasions, he could not find the right ones. However, whatever little he found was prepared and Mzee Ng'iti would use it for a few days. Sakagwa, being an obedient son, continued to treat his father using all the knowledge and herbs he had learnt. But as luck would have it, Mzee Ng'iti succumbed to illness as his son administered treatment.

Although he did not heal his first patient, Sakagwa had gathered a whale of knowledge from his deceased father. Later, he would use this knowledge extensively where many people with diverse ailments from all over Gusii came to his home for remedies. Others would seek advice from him on various aspects of life and illness. Still others sought interpretation of visions of certain situations and events that confronted them.

In the next subsections, we discuss some of the ways Sakagwa acted as a medicine man in the community.

Herbal Treatment

Sakagwa treated most of his patients using plant extracts which utilize different parts of a plant. Depending on the ailment, specific parts of specific plants - flowers, leaves, roots, and the bark - could be used.

Whatever part was used, the typical process was to boil it to release the medicinal extracts. In some cases the plants were dried and burnt to ashes which was then used for medicinal purposes.

The means of administration were various. There are cases where the extracts were taken orally or, in case of external injury the extract was applied on the surface of the ailment. For those taken orally, the medicine man could recommend ingestion with (say) animal – chicken, goat, etc. - soup

Sakagwa also dispensed herbal medicine in another manner. He prepared ashes from roots and leaves of certain herbs. Such was then mixed with hot water and drank or applied directly to the ailing part of the body.

Also, there were cases where Sakagwa's medicines were used to 'forestall' the actions of an enemy. Such medicine would be taken with the express belief that the intermediary spirits would kill members of the offending clan or community, through disease or any disaster. In some case, the medicines were believed to drive the enemy insane, kill their cattle, ruin their crops or afflict them with pestilence.

> **Editor's Note:** *this last aspect is similar to the concept of* ebiranya *captured in the next subsection.*

Ebiranya & Protection from Harm at War

During the many wars between the Kipsigis and the people of North Mugirango, Sakagwa is said to have assisted the Gusii community realize victory in a number of these battles.

In traditional Gusii society, there is a concept of *ebiranya,* a special magical concoction believed to have an effect on a subject to who it pertains. As warriors planned to face the enemy, Sakagwa could prepare the *ebiranya* from a mixture of specific leaves, barks from particular trees and roots of certain plants. Those who needed help were made to drink this concoction. They believed that the *ebiranya* had magical powers that would protect them against any harm and hence enable them beat the enemy.

There is more that Sakagwa did beyond *ebiranya*. He could get leaves, barks and roots from diverse but specific plants. He would then mix and burn them into ashes. Before any war, warriors were made to smear their bodies with this ash, in the belief that no weapon could harm them[1].

There is another dimension to the *ebiranya* as applied by Sakagwa. Before going to war, the sage

---

1 **Editor's Note:** *this is similar to the Maji Maji rebellion in present-day Tanzania where resistance to colonial rule show warriors smear themselves in such concoctions believing that bullets could not kill them.*

would put sticks on the ground, and using his seer paraphernalia, he could 'read' the outcomes of the impending battle. This way, he could give valuable advice to the people. This advice enabled the warriors to win many battles.

As always, while going through these processes, Sakagwa invoked the spirits of *chisokoro* on whose behalf he was administering the 'treatment' or prescribing a course of action.

For warriors, the net effect was that of taking an oath. The implication was that they committed to fight gallantly to protect the community and protect their fellow warriors from harm in the battlefield. A key element of the 'oath' dealt with betrayal; anyone betraying the cause of the war, their fellow warriors and protection of the community would have a curse unto himself and his offspring.

> **Editor's Note:** *One can argue that, as much as science does not explicitly support the theory of* ebiranya, *the fact is that those involved believed in its effectiveness. It can be claimed that this was a form of psychological conditioning that galvanized the warriors and made them fight believing they were protected and that they were destined to win.*
>
> *All these types of treatment gave the warriors encouragement and new inspiration to fight with all their strength.*

Process of Treatment

Sakagwa had a ritualistic way of adminstering treatment. Before he dispensed medicines, he took time to instil in his patients the spirit of worship through **chisokoro**. He made his subjects understand that the importance of believing in the ancesors's intevervention for one to heal. This is in line with Gusii spirituality where *chisokoro* co-existed with the people in the Gusii conception of one Supreme Being, *Engoro.*

Sakagwa always advised his clients, that it was important for them to ask for blessings from *Engoro* through *chisokoro*. This was done typically before going for war or undertaking any critical tasks. It was through *chisokoro* that *Engoro* communicated his message to the living, Sakagwa taught.

All these notwithstanding, medicine men were largely concerned with sickness and misfortunes, which were generally believed to be caused by the ill-will or ill-action of one person against another. The latter related particularly to the agency of witchcraft and magic. The medicine man's duty was therefore to discover the cause of the illness and offer the proper treatment.

In addition, once the medicine man had diagnosed the nature of the disease, he needed to apply the right treatment and put in place a means of preventing the recurrence of the disease. In the case of suspected ill-will, the medicine man's task was identify the culprit and pronounce the right remedy to prevent further harm from the evil-leaning person.

To some extent, medicine men in Gusii follow this process even today when dealing with illnesses and misfortunes. It is partly psychological and partly physical. The medicine man treats the ailment using herbs. Spiritually, he assures the sufferer that all will be well and supported by *chisokoro* and *Engoro*. This then engenders belief that all will be well in the end. The medicine man, in modern jargon, was in effect both a doctor and a 'pastor' to the sick person.

In most cases, Sakagwa dispensed medicines for free, or charged very little. He took his role as a calling from *Engoro* and *chisokoro* and as a duty to the community. In the end, this earned him the love of not only the people of Gusii but also of foreigners, including Luos, Maasais and Kipsigis.

Sakagwa as Rainmaker and Diviner

Droughts were a very common phenomenon in Gusii of the time, at least from the stories passed down generations. When they happened, they caused devastation as crops withered, and livestock died due to lack of pastures. The result was loss of livestock and famine that could claim many lives of people.

When bad things happened to Abagusii, they reasoned that *chisokoro* and *Engoro* may not be happy with them. The people could typically visit a seer to advise them on the cause of the calamity and the way out of the misfortune. The seer would then prescribe a remedy to address the situation. Typical remedies were sacrifices offered to appease *chisokoro* and *Engoro*. These rituals were typically accompanied by various forms of activities, including dances and the like.

In Gusii society of the time, rainmakers[2] played a very important role in dealing with issues of drought and rain. They were intercessors for the community who came into action following protracted droughts.

Sakagwa, like his father before him, performed this important role of a rainmaker in the

---

2 **Editor's Note:** it is possible that rainmakers truly understood the key signs of coming rain, like present-day meteorologists and timed the *ribina* to happen just at the crux of it raining.

community. Whenever there was a prolonged drought, people would come to him for assistance in predicting when it would rain. They would ask him to intercede, on their behalf, with the *chisokoro* and *Engoro*. Here, he would then organize and bring together groups of women to stage the rain dance, *ribina*[3].

Women in traditional regalia would gather at a specific point and stage the dance as the rest of the community watched.

Indeed, after they had danced for a day or two, rain would fall in torrents. At times, it would rain before the women got to their homes following the *ribina*.

On the other hand, there are times when there was too much rainfall or when it 'rained' hailstones that destroyed crops. As with the drought, Sakagwa would be called upon to intervene. Accordingly, he would organize people to perform rituals as mediation measures that would slow down the destruction.

---

3 **Editor's Note:** for a detailed description of the role of *ribina* in Gusii community, see J. S. Akama's *The Gusii of Kenya: Social, Economic, Cultural, Political & Judicial Perspectives* (Nsemia Inc, 2017).

Omogoroka O' Sakagwa

This is a type of cactus (*euphorbia ingens*), called *engoto* in Ekegusii under which the sage held court. It was found in Bogeka clan in Bogetutu at Gesoni hill. Under this tree, Sakagwa made and dispensed medicines, including *ebiranya*. In short, the area around and under tree acted as Sakagwa's clinic where he attended to his clients. Many of his prophecies were also pronounced here. It was believed that anybody who had evil charms or who was a cattle rustler, a witch or wizard could not pass under this sacred tree lest they face the wrath of chisokoro.

In addition, it is here that Sakagwa conducted rainmaking activities. Women and young ladies would come where the tree is located for traditional ceremonies like *amabina* following prolonged droughts. The dances were meant to appease *Engoro* and *chisokoro* to bring rain. This ritual of ribina happened almost annually

Sakagwa as a Community Sage

As a community wise man, Sakagwa dispensed many pieces of advice depending on who came to him for counsel. Some people would come to seek advice on various aspects of life and illness. Still others sought interpretation of visions of certain situations and events that confronted them.

That said, Sakagwa focused on community issues. He was oftentimes frustrated by the lack of unity among the clans of Gusii. Frequently, the inter-clan skirmishes led to unnecessary loss with the overall effect of weakening the entire Omogusii. He advocated for internal understanding and dispute resolution so as to enhance collective understanding and investment in collective strength.

To address such issues, he often called clan leaders for discussions on how to resolve the issues. In some cases others called upon him to advise on what to do with dilemmas they faced.

In playing this role, Sakagwa acted selflessly and dispensed advice based on the overarching interest of the community. A key plank of his advice was communal unity and purposeful cooperation that would strengthen Abagusii. Being strong internally, he reasoned, would assure they would face external aggression from a point of strength.

Given his actions, Sakagwa gained trust with many heads of clans and warriors, and, indeed, even other ethnic groups. As such his stature and respect grew to such an extent that it placed him in a position where he could summon parties for counsel when a need arose.

For this purpose, he had a place outside his homestead, under a tree, where he held court. As we will see later, such power enabled him to assemble a large number of people at his home for his 'farewell' party, the 'Last Supper'!

It is noteworthy that Sakagwa, due to pure influence, was the first person to bring a modicum of unity among the various clans of Gusii. The impact of this power of uniting people would manifest itself when Abagusii faced the Kipsigis in the epic battle of Osaosao.

Sakagwa – the Prophet

Over and above all the medicines dispensed, rainmaking dances convened and counsel given, Sakagwa played the role of a seer by dispensing prophetic pronouncements to the community. In this role, every word that came from his mouth was taken seriously and all instructions he gave were, to a great extent, obeyed to the letter. In a way, it was because of his constant affirmation to his audience that every word he uttered came from *Engoro*, God, through *chisokoro*.

We have seen how, as a young person, during the several skirmishes between the Kipsigis and the people of North Mugirango, Sakagwa made several trips to the area of conflict. He could stay there for a while on each of those trips. His mission, word passed down generations has it, was to try to make peace between the warring parties.

When the wars subsided, Sakagwa moved to Mwamosioma and got married to his first wife, Kerubo. At Mwamosioma, he continued to practise his trade, dispensing medicines and making prophecies.

Towards the middle of 1880s, there were recurrent droughts and famines in Gusiil. Sakagwa is said to have told people that *Engoro* and the *chisokoro* were not happy with the people because of their many transgressions. He warned that because Abagusii were no longer following the traditions and customs of their forefathers as required by tradition, calamities would not cease. Many people, especially those from his clan of Bogeka[4], called him mad. Others protested by burning down his homestead.

Despite these violent and hostile reactions by some of his people, Sakagwa did not change his resolve of pointing a wagging finger at them.

In this section we give an overview of his well-known prophesies.

4 **Editor's Note:** *this is a case of a prophet having no respect in his home!*

Warning about Locusts & Famine

Around the year 1886, Sakagwa announced that because Abagusii had refused to listen to the demands of their ancestral spirits, the area they ocupied would be faced with devastation. It would be invaded by a swarm of locusts (*orong'ang'a*) after which there would follow a drought and a dreadful famine, he said. Few people, especially from his clan, took this warning seriously.

Sure to Sakagwa's word, in the year 1888, Gusiil was invaded by huge swarms of locusts. These ravaging insects thoroughly devastated all vegetation, including crops that were still in the fields.

The following year, there was unprecedented drought. It is said that the countryside was so dry that hundreds of wild animals, particularly elephants, roamed all over Gusii in search of water. Because the previous years (1888) crops had been destroyed by locusts, the year 1889 saw a terrible famine generally remembered as the famine of *enyamakongiro*. At this time, the people were subjected to eating green leaves of any plant they could lay their hands on. *Rikongiro* (wandering Jew), a drought resistant vegetable - a creeper - grows wildly. It is not usually eaten by Abagusii who have plenty of other vegetable types to live on. However, this time round they were forced to eat *rikongiro* because it was the only green vegetable that was available and it was not harmful to their health.

As if the locust invasion and the drought that followed were not enough, in the same year, 1889, East Coast Fever struck hard, killing large herds of cattle and other livestock. Without cattle from which to get milk, especially for feeding children, this calamity presented an existential crisis. Many Gusii mothers resorted to the unthinkable, albeit inevitable, move to help save their children. They could barter their children for food from the Kipsigis and the Luo to ensure that the children survived. In return, the families receiveed food such as grains, usually millet or *wimbi,* to feed the rest of the members of their families.

With this famine and livestock that was all but wiped out, people resorted to cooking dried animal skins/hides in place of meat!

To make it worse, the Maasai and the Kipsigis are said to have stepped up their cattle raiding activities all over Gusii during this terrible period.

People who survived the famine of *enyamakongiro* and the subsequent death of their livestock remembered the words Sakagwa had uttered before the advent of the calamities: reform or else you will face the wrath of *Engoro* and *chisokoro*!

The Case of 'Amandegere' at Getembe

With the end of the famine and subsequent wipe-out of livestock due to East Coast Fever, some people realized the importance of Sakagwa's words. He attracted enemies and friends almost in equal measure, with some associating his name with bad omen for the community. It appeared like he had a penchant for predicting the worst, albeit with a message of hope, and which worst came to pass!

Sensing his life to be in danger, he decided to act. This is when he migrated to Sengera on the boundary of Bobasi and Machoge. On arrival at the place, he realized his reputation had preceded him. The people there had already heard about him, his words and actions. They reacted in a similar manner as those he was running away from had reacted. He could not stay there for long because the same trouble between the people and himself started all over again. When the people there refused to listen to him, he warned them of dire consequences.

As some of them planned to kill him, he escaped in the night and headed to Kiong'anyo near present-day Kisii Town. It is said that the people who had planned to kill him were killed by lions as they pursued him. To this day, there are many who believe his pursuers died because of he cursed them.

From Kiong'anyo, Sakagwa moved to Kanyimbo, where he stayed for some time. His area of operations, with Kanyimbo as his base, was Getembe, present-day Kisii Town. He continued making pronouncements according to word passed down generations.

It is reported that, one day, he collected a lot of rats and carried them in baskets to the central place in Getembe, the site where the District Commissioner's (DC's) offices were later built. Here he opened the baskets in which he had carried the rodents. All the rats started running in different directions. Some people, who had followed him, wondered where he was taking the rats or what he was going to do with them. He told the people that in days to come, there will be a lot of *amandegere* (a form of edible mushrooms) in this place. The 'people with sons' will enjoy life as their sons will enable them 'harvest the mushrooms'; those 'without sons' would have little of it.

Many believe that Sakagwa's utterances had a deeper meaning. By mushrooms, they argue, he meant new forms of wealth other than livestock. And by the term 'those with sons', the interpretation goes, he meant those parents with educated children. As such only those with children who have an education would enjoy life while those without educated children would suffer a great deal.

Many people in Gusii believe that this has come to pass! Livestock as a form of wealth is no longer a big deal. Yet, education and other things that are consequences of education, now symbolize wealth and wellbeing.

The Case of the Coming of Kisii Town

Around the same time as he was pronouncing *amandegere naame Getembe*, Sakagwa called a group of Kisii elders to Getembe. Here he made another prophecy demonstrated by action. He started by lighting a fire from present-day Daraja Mbili to Kisii High School, all along. Apparently, it is the line along which electric poles that light the town follow.

He went further and indicated places of new contraptions that ended up being the police lines, the hospital, the offices and the churches would be in a future that is presently in Kisii Town.

Obviously, it was difficult for those present to imagine electric poles when they had seen none and knew not of anything to do with electricity. It was impossible for them to make out the rest of the details – police lines, the hospital, offices and churches, etc. – that was beyond their imagination.

Over the years, though, what he predicted has come to pass and hence the realization of what he meant.

The Coming of White People

Another time Sakagwa made another famous prediction. He told the people that "one day people with child-like skins (white) will come who will bring different forms of government and laws". The foreigners, he said, would have 'fire smoking pipes' (guns) that can kill! As such, he warned the Gusii warriors that they would be disarmed by the strangers if they showed resistance. He told them that these strangers would stay and later leave for their country, leaving us to rule ourselves the way we were in the past.

When the people heard about all these things they thought that Sakagwa was day dreaming because they had never even heard of the existence of people with 'child-like' skins – white people. Only a few years passed and then white men from Tanzania, Arabs, reached Kisii territory. Abagusii called these Arab traders *Abarumbasi*.

The white men came in earnest in 1905 and started their invasion (led by soldiers of the Kings African Rifles, KAR) of Gusii approaching the territory from Karungu. They faced resistance and many, on either side, lost their lives. They retreated and sought reinforcements.

They would arrive 'better prepared' and hence fully armed in 1907. They fought fiercely with Gusii warriors led by Otenyo Nyamaterere. In some instance, Otenyo speared and wounded Geoffrey Alexander Northcote, the District Commissioner in Kisii. Sensing that Abagusii would lose more people, clan elders sought a truce to which the white man demanded the surrender of Otenyo. The warrior would later be beheaded and (reportedly) his head sent to England.

Other Prophecies

Of Wars and the Triumph of the Black Person

At Gesoni, Sakagwa made another prophecy. He told people of the Bogeka clan of Bogetutu that there will be three forms of struggle for power, saying that during the 3rd campaign, the black man will win.

Many that have thought about and interpreted this believe they understood what he meant. They believe he meant that the black man would be victorious in the 3rd campaign.

There was a first war (World War I) and the black man did not gain anything; then there was the second war (World War II) and again the black man did not win, the third war is the war of independence where the white man was uprooted and his rule came to an end.

Of Parents, Children and Grandchildren

In another prophecy, Sakagwa spoke of parents, their children and grandchildren. He said that 'he who will have a son will have a grandson and the grandson will not be the same'.

This puzzled people who wondered how progeny could be different from the parent. However, some have interpreted this to mean that things will change with time. They say that it means that, because of changes and social transformation, children and grandchildren would live different kinds of lives. For example, children and grandchildren would be better educated than their fathers or grandfathers.

This is happening today, what with formal education, different livings styles and rapid changes in technology.

Some Observations on Sakagwa's Prophecies

While Sakagwa was busy pronouncing all these prophecies, many people in the community were dying from famine and pestilence. Many faced war, exposed to the cruel spears of Kipsigis warriors on cattle raiding missions. When consulted about all these tribulations, Sakagwa approached the matters from a spiritual disposition. Accordingly, he communicated with the ancestral spirits (*chisokoro*) using his magical paraphernalia that had been passed down generations.

On one such occasion, following his communication with *chisokoro*, Sakagwa led a group of elders to Manga Ridge where they performed sacrifices at the graves of Oisera and Nyakundi. Remember Oisera was the father of Nyakundi who in turn was the father of Abagetutu.

After this, Sakagwa came back and urged the elders and the community to always observe established customs and to continually remember our ancestors whom many of them had abandoned. It is said that, on that very day, it rained heavily and for the next four years there was unprecedented heavy rainfall all over Gusii resulting in bumper harvests.

Such an act of guiding the community in the face of troubles elevated Sakagwa's stature in the community even more.

Throughout his time and interactions with the people, Sakagwa never claimed to 'own' the messages he brought to the community. He always indicated that he was only a medium for transmission of the messages from *Engoro* through *chisokoro* to the people. The manifestation of his predictions and advice made Sakagwa even more popular to many. The result: he was not only sought for his medicinal knowledge and treatment but also the advice he dispensed in the process.

We believe that Sakagwa was prophet in so far as he satisfied the anxieties of his age, and also in so far as he was occasionally impelled by external powers to articulate messages of more general and fundamental importance and indeed to pronounce principles and norms that were critical during his time.

In Gusii, Sakagwa stands out as a beacon like no other. It is possible to call him a prophet but he also qualifies as a philosopher (in a strict sense) among the community of Abagusii and their neighbours. With thorough examination, he could easily pass for a Plato, Socrates or some other such philosophers from other societies. Many of these philosophers rightly understood and believed that man's organic life cannot last forever. As such, as Aristotle would have it, 'man's true end is happiness', which can only be attained by the fullest development of one's true rational nature. As such, cultivation of intellectual and moral values is essential for fulfilment of one's 'mission' on earth. Sakagwa showed intellectual depth beyond the average person of his time. He was a sage philosopher in the context of Odera Oruka's definition[5].

There are many pronouncements that Sakagwa made but because they did not stand out as those presented here, it is impossible to recount all of them. These other pronouncements did not

---

5 H. Odera Oruka, *Sage Philosophy: The Basic Question*, in *Sage Philosophy: Indigenous Thinkers and Modern Debate on African Philosophy*, ed. H. Odera Oruka, E. J. Brill, 1990

acquire prominence as those enuncitated here.

For example, while living at Kanyimbo, but operating at Getembe, Sakagwa continued making pronouncements. He did this even as he went about dispending medicines, including *ebiranya.*

At the core of his message to leaders of Abagusii was unity amongst themselves as leaders as a basis for unity in the community.

> **Editor's Note:** *In* The Untold Story of the Gusii of Kenya: Survival Techniques and Resistance to the Establishment of British Colonial Rule, *Prof. John Akama captures the coming of the white colonial government in Gusii and the white man's incursion into Getembe. He writes about the resistance by Gusii warriors led to Otenyo Nyamaterere. On arrival in Gusii, British soldiers (the Kings African Rifles) met stiff resistance staged by Gusii warriors. Although they lost fewer soldiers than the number of warriors killed, the KAR beat a retreat to regroup.*
>
> *They would later attack two years later and finally pacify Abagusii. In this encounter, Otenyo speared Alexander Northcote, the colonial administrator, following which there was wanton massacre of Abagusii. Only when the elders felt the community might be exterminated did they persuade Otenyo to surrender, having been promised by the colonial officers that nothing will happen to the warrior. Otenyo would later surrender, be captured, decapitated and his torso buried on the present-day grounds of Kisii Sports Club. It is said that his head was sent to the UK. Lately, Gusii elders have made demands for the return of Otenyo's head for proper burial as would befit such a hero of Abagusii*
>
> *Some people see the resistance against colonial incursion as having gone against Sakagwa's advice. The question is: would the calamity of death of many young people in the hail of bullets from the*

guns of KAR soldiers have been avoided?

Fast forward to 1963 and Kenya got independence from Britain. With that, the white man left the country and we started managing our affairs.

Was this Sakagwa's prophecy coming true? The triumph of the black person third time around?

Sakagwa the Strategist and the Battle of Osaosao

Stories passed down generations capture Sakagwa's uniqueness in many ways, some of which have been covered in the previous sections. The stories tell of a person who seemed be on a mission in service of the community. It is in this respect that he devoted a lot of time and efforts to the unity of Abagusii.

We believe that this focus was informed, in part, by lessons he learnt in going about his work. For example, in North Mugirango, he fought side by side with Abagusii warriors to ward off attacks from Kipsigis raiders. In the process, he learnt and understood war techniques that enabled the warriors resist being overrun by invaders.

Sakagwa was also widely travelled in dispensing medicines in Gusii and territories of neighbouring ethnic groups: the Maasai, the Luo and the Kipsigis. Clearly, these sojourns gave him an advantage of insights into these communities and Gusii clans that many of his age did not have. Such insights could include the psychological dispositions of the people, their various strengths and weakness.

As well, combined with these experiences were lessons from his father and the old man's demise.

One can deduce that he learnt that even when one does one's best, one can lose the battle in the end. Sakagwa had worked in treating his father using the best known techniques and medicines learnt from his father but passed down generations. In the end, he lost the battle and his father succumbed to illness.

It appears that all this influenced his thinking to focus on service to the community. As discussed elsewhere, one could term him an 'abundant thinker', more disposed to giving than receiving.

It is with this backdrop that he would participate in, perhaps, the most defining moment regarding the survival of Abagusii as a community. The battle of Osaosao[6], fought between Abagusii and the Kipsigis, was brutal and cost a lot of lives of Kipsigis warriors. It is permanently edged in stories that are told in the two communities, perhaps underlining its emotional impact on the two communities. It would be the last major clash between Abagusii and their Kipsigis neighbours.

*****

After the different Gusii clans had taken up their different settlements across the land of Gusii, they put in place traditional systems for protection against enemies. Specifically, around their homesteads, they had trenching and fortification (*chindwaki*) as a means of defense, including around the encampments, *ebisarate*. They also organized contingencies of warriors for rapid response against attacks, many of who were trained in their days at *ebisarate*.

Despite all these defense mechanisms, warriors

---

6 Abagusii call this *Esegi y'Egetonto*! (the war fought in the marshes); the Kipsigis know it as *Saosao*.

from enemy ethnic groups remained a dangerous menace to Abagusii as they continually encroached on Gusii territory and raided homesteads to take livestock almost at will.

It is noteworthy that the Kipsigis were majorly interested in cattle and land for pasture. However, whenever they attacked, they left behind a wave of destruction and a devastated people. Aside from cattle and women, they carried away all kinds of food and, as they left, burnt houses and cut into pieces all old or weak livestock which could not be hurriedly driven away.

While all this was happening, Sakagwa's fame as a seer and medicine man had become widespread all over Gusii and beyond. His stature loomed large and prominent community elders seemed to recognize this.

It is in this respect that elders Kimaiga, Ogaro and Nyakundi[7] led a delegation of fellow elders to meet with Sakagwa. We estimate that this took place around years of 1889 and 1891. The objective was to craft a way forward in dealing with the constant raids and their subsequent devastating impact on the community. Sakagwa

---

7 **Editor's Note:** *In* The Gusii of Kenya: Social, Economic, Cultural, Political & Judicial Perspectives, *Prof. John Akama indicates that part of the concern of the elders went farther back in history than with the persistent raids by the Kipsigis warriors. Abagusii had been uprooted from Trans Mara by the Maasai a number of decades earlier, something that happened after their leader Ongarora was felled by the Maasai. Lack of unity saw Abagusii dispersal where some ended up in Kuria while most trekked back to present day Gusii. As part of the oath and war preparations for Osaosao, Abagusii swore never to have a repeat of Ngarora, the war with the Maasai in Trans Mara.*

chaired the meeting.

First they agreed that whenever the Kipsigis or Maasai warriors were sighted in Gusii, alarms would be raised, horns would be blown and word sent around so that all community warriors could come out to confront the common enemy.

Second, given Sakagwa's capability to foretell things, he was tasked to keep the people of Gusii well informed of the tell-tale signs of possible attacks and, if possible, the actual day the Kipsigis or the Maasai would strike.

This was the start of the preparations for the war or battle of Osaosao that happened in 1893.

After the meeting with the elders, Ogaro, Nyakundi and Kimaiga together, with the leaders of the others Gusii clans, Sakagwa is said to have gone secretly to consult *hisokoro* at *Ngoro ya Mwaga* at the base of the Manga Ridge. This is a place at bottom of Manga ridge where the graves of ancestors like Oisera and Nyakundi are believed to be found.

It is said that Sakagwa stayed at the place for two consecutive nights communicating with *chisokoro*. He also performed rituals that were meant to appease the spirits as was the tradition of the day.

When he had done all these, he came back home and summoned Nyakundi, Kimaiga and Ogaro and together they took a collective oath, committing their people to go to war while united. They averred that they would face the attackers, be they the Kipisigis or Maasai, as one people with coordinated action. Ogaro, Nyakundi, Kimaiga and other elders were tasked with going to their respective clan councils and relaying the message. It was even more pertinent, Sakagwa told them, because of an impending war against the Kipsigis.

> **Editor's Note:** *Abagusii believe that, aside from the rituals at Ngoro ya 'Mwaga, Sakagwa also planted ebiranya under Omote o'Sakagwa. Along with the oath all elders took, he got an iron-clad commitment that the warriors, with the force of clan unity behind them, would fight as one force. And ebiranya had the magical-spiritual effect of ensuring all towed the line, lest they be cursed along with their progeny.*

It is said that when the Kipsigis received wind that Sakagwa had united the various Abagusii divisions against them, they kept off all raiding missions into Gusii. This pause lasted for a while and, except for a few thieving expeditions in North Mugirango, their raids were all but absent.

In the history of Abagusii, this was the only time members of the community were totally united. As one Langat, writing on Facebook in 2020, rightly put it, the battle of Osaosao is considered to be a turning point in survival of Abagusii. Abagusii warriors, with Sakagwa's blessings, were instructed to wait till they were given an appropriate signal on how and where to start their attacks. They stayed waiting; fully prepared.

THE GIANT FIG TREE (OMOGUMO[8])

The fig tree was located at Boking'oina in Kitutu Chache North. Various cultural festivals were organized here.

The Gusii prophet Sakagwa, administered cleansing and applied protective charms to those who were confronted by enemies. It is here also that Sakagwa planted magical charms (*ebiranya*) that enabled Gusii warriors defeat invading Kipsigis warriors during the historical battle of Osaosao.

*****

Meanwhile, between 1888 and 1892, a cattle disease called *ong'ong'o* (rinderpest) swept through the Luo, Gusii and Kipsigis territories, killing hundreds of thousands of heads of cattle in its wake. Abagusii recall that the disease, which broke out initially in Luoland, first made cattle go blind before they died. For the Kipsigis

---

8   Only an example; the original fig tree has long been cut down the unfortunate march of deforestation progresses.

who depended on cattle more than Abagusii or the Luo, this was devastating. As such, finding themselves with very few cattle, they organized a huge raid into Gusii to replenish their stocks.

From tales passed down generations, it appears that the Kipsigis thoroughly prepared for this expedition. They were sure of victory as it had mostly happened in the past. This is in spite of the knowledge of the unity and preparedness of Abagusii mediated by Sakagwa. It is further reported, again from folklore passed down Abagusii generations, that the Kipsigis enlisted young boys who would drive captured livestock home. Unverified[9] reports suggest that, in their party, they planned to have even women who would carry home food collected following a successful. Little did they know they would meet their Waterloo!

Reports indicate that the well-heeled Kipsigis contingent set off from Sotik. It was a force to scare anyone. At its head was one Malabun Arap Makiche of Sotik. Another leader, Chesengeny arap Kaborok had a contingent that teamed with Makiche's at Buret, according to a Facebook page post by one Arap Langat.

Editor's Note: *My grandmother used to talk about this war and specifically the leader of the Kipsigis warriors, who she said was left-handed (nyakebee) and whose mother was herself Omogusii. For some reason, this Nyakebee hated Abagusii like hell but*

---

9 We use the term 'unverified' here because there is no evidence that Kipsigis women actually appeared in the battle, either killed or captured. As well, there is no evidence that young boys were in the party either. Abagusii folklore speaks of self-confident warriors in large number rampaging through Gusii and later waylaid and killed in their numbers.

> *was also out to prove a point and bring home cattle to help restock Kipsigis herds. Nyakebee (arap Makiche it turns out and who also had a mother from Gusii) chose to go to war despite warnings from their seer, the Olkoiyot who perhaps having understood the preparations Abagusii had made and the fact that Abagusii were fed up with such raids, had warned the warriors that the war would not be in their favour. ... Nyakebee could not hear of it and chose to go to war all the same. History has the results for all to see.*

It is clear that the Kipsigis warriors were sure of victory despite caution from their elders and seer. For the hot-blooded young men, it appeared to be the question of 'when' rather than 'if' they will conquer Abagusii and come home with herds of cattle.

They started their march to expected victory one afternoon, reaching the banks of River Gucha in the evening. It is reported that, as they advanced into Gusii, they cited vultures[10]. We learn that the presence of vultures when one is headed for war or an important mission is a bad omen in the Kipsigis belief system.

It said that, sensing that something was amiss, Arap Kaborok raised concerns and suggested they abort the mission. He tried, in vain, to persuade Arap Makiche to abandon the raid that was underway. Fuelled by Arap Makiche's determination, Arap Kaborok's warriors abandoned him, calling him a coward and followed Makiche.

The raid started in North Mugirango and ended at Manga. In raiders' estimation, it was very successful. As was the case with many such

---

10 Abagusii believe it was Sakagwa who sent the scavengers.

previous raids, many Gusii villages were destroyed and a large number of livestock captured.

However, at Manga, things started going wrong for the ever-confident invaders. A difference of opinion arose between the two warrior leaders. Arap Makiche decided that they continue with the raid into Luoland to get even more 'loot'. Arap Kaborok's disagreed and, with his followers in tow, headed back home via Maasai territory.

*****

All this time, the Gusii elders, their clan councils and warriors were patient and confident; they were waiting for the right time and signal to strike as planned. The order would come from Sakagwa and the other elders. They believed that in these preparations, Sakagwa knew exactly what was happening and that he had prepared, blessed and alerted the community warriors accordingly. Many believe that, as the Gusii prophet, Sakagwa knew that the battle of Osaosao would be a defining moment for the survival of Abagusii as a community.

As the Arap Makiche-led Kipsigis warrior contingent was headed to Luoland, Abagusii began raising alarms as trained. They blew horns and beat their drums of war as trained before. Runners, with tacit messages, were sent from Kitutu to all parts of Gusii: Nyaribari, North Mugirango, Bobasi, Machoge, South Mugirango and Bonchari. Gusii warriors, on receiving the news, hurried to Manga. Here, they waylaid the Kipsigis warriors who would be on their way back from their raid in Luoland

By the early hours of the critical day, the Kitutu, Bassi, Machoge, Nyaribari and Mugirango forces had taken position at the eastern side of the Manga escarpment, ready for ambush.

The Luos were not 'sleeping' either! At the dawn of the critical day, they chased the now tired Kipsigis warriors from Mumbo. When the fleeing Kipsigis warriors reached the Manga escarpment, and as they ascended along the valley of River Charachani, they came face to face with the Gusii warriors. Caught between the Luo from the back and Gusii warriors in front of them, the Kipsigis had few options left. That day, the Kipsigis raiders who were now surrounded, were killed to a man.

According to accounts by Abagusii, the water of the Charachani River turned crimson due to the slashed and bleeding bodies of the Kipsigis warriors which were thrown into it. Gusii lore has it that, as the battle raged, some Kipsigis warriors would attempt to hide themselves in the marshes along the river from which they were ferreted in no time. Others pretended to be dead by covering themselves with the blood and the insides of the dead. But the Gusii warriors did not take any chances. They would confirm, one by one, whether all the Kipsigis were indeed dead. They did this by stabbing bodies with spears. When they discovered that some of the Kipsigis raiders, that were pretending to be dead, reacted with anguish at such pain, the Gusii warriors cut the bodies and the injured, who had feigned death, into small pieces.

In their history, Abagusii had never achieved such a victory over any of their enemies. They therefore became extremely elated. They named the bloody battle as the Battle of Osaosao or *Esegi y'Egetonto* (the War that was fought in marshland). As a matter of fact, it is argued that if it were not for Sakagwa, who had united Abagusii, used his medicine and foresight with respect to preparations, Abagusii would not have accomplished such a feat.

As each Gusii group left the battle field, they garlanded themselves with leaves and sang merrily as they trotted home. The victory of Osaosao further immortalized Sakagwa's name.

*****

The battle was a major setback for the Kipsigis. Many of those that died in battle were young men who were transiting to family life. Many of them were ready for marriage. With so many dead, the question was how to perpetuate family lineages. Worse still, with so many young men dead, there was an excess of would be brides. The elders needed a way out of the mess.

In the Kipsigis culture of the time, for a man to get married, he must have undergone proper rites of passage into adulthood that included circumcision. To deal with this predicament, Kipsigis community elders ordered the initiation of young boys ahead of their time. They also encouraged the boys to marry earlier than would have been the case so as to perpetuate the lineage of their tribe.

> **Editor's Note:** (a) *unverified accounts suggest that some of the 'beneficiaries' of this Kipsigis dilemma were adult Gusii men. These moved in and settled with Kipsigis women with who they started families. Effectively, they became part of the Kipsigis.* (b) *the war was the last one fought between Abagusii and the Kipsigis. Soon, colonialism came and the white people claimed border lands between the two ethnic groups as part of the White Highlands. This became a buffer where the two could not interact easily.*

Sakagwa in Old Age & Death

At Gesoni near *Chisokoro*

As indicated previously, by the time Sakagwa came to settle at Gesoni, he was already an old man. This was in late 1890s, a very troubled period in Gusii history when the community was trying to find their permanent settlement.

The community knew no peace as it was being harassed from all directions by their hostile neighbours. On the one hand there were the Maasai while on the other were the Kipsigis.

Sakagwa believed that *chisokoro* sought him out to articulate their wishes to the erring people of Gusii. As such, he continually laboured to point the way out of their problems. According to him what Abagusii specifically needed at the time was unity, unity to defend themselves against constant harassment and attack, unity to act as a people in the interest of collective security and unity of purpose underlined by respect for *Engoro* and *chisokoro*. As such, he constantly warned the people against petty differences and about their impending doom, unless they heeded his warnings. For him, the problems in Gusii (the drought, pestilences and ethnic wars with enemy tribes) were the direct judgment of *Engoro* and *chisokoro* on religious, political and social failures.

It is around this time that he eventually convinced Abagusii clan elders to unite; unity that led to victory over the Kipsigis in the battle of Osaosao.

At Gesoni, he continued with more activities – prophesying, dispensing medicines for ailments and holding court with other elders. It is here that he pronounced that the black man would win in the 3rd attempt. It is also here that he spoke of education when he said that 'he who will have a son will have a grandson and the grandson will not stay the same'.

It is reported that he was also embroiled in clan conflicts, perhaps feeling the injustice inflicted upon his people of Bogeka clan[1]. Apparently, community lore suggests, he instigated a sub-clan fight between the people of Bogeka (Abageka) and Bogusero (Abagusero). The fight was over land and Abagusero wanted more of the land occupied by Abageka for farming and grazing livestock.

The battleground was where Riotero Seventh Day Adventist (SDA) School stands today. In the clash, Abagusero fought with all their might, led by their leader Ombati but they were no match to the well-prepared Abageka. It is said that when Ombati sensed defeat, he ran off to Kisumu to curry favour with and seek the support of the white man, whom they had heard of. In those days, there were neither roads nor vehicles to Kisumu as such Ombati walked all the way to Kisumu in the company of his close-knit advisors and clansmen.

As Ombati was seeking external help, the fighting continued with Abagusero suffering defeat where they were pushed to the present boundary between the two clans, and the place where Cardinal Otunga High School stands today.

---

[1] He we can see that Sakagwa was also not above clan disunity; lessons from such clashes, especially their futility, could have informed his initiatives to create unity among clans.

*****

Watching the events surrounding Sakagwa's last days leads many to believe that he felt and saw his death coming. It was around the early 1900s and he was advancing in age. He was now firmly settled at Gesoni, a place close to where his ancestors (especially those of Bogeka clan) were interred.

With advancing age, it came a time when he was not able to travel around Gusii as he used to. This time, those who wanted his services would come to his Gesoni home. Leaders, especially, sought his knowledge and counsel. People seeking treatment would come for medicines.

As well, due to his fame which went beyond Gusii, Sakagwa would receive and attend to people from among the Kipsigis, the Maasai and the Luo. Not only were his medicines potent, his words of counsel and predictions could be relied upon to be effective. They were also affordable. It is said that there were times he chose not to charge any fees for the services, especially in situations that appeared desperate.

*****

Take note that, initially, Sakagwa's message to Abagusii faced resistance. It brought him nothing but opposition, hatred and persecution. Only after the fulfillment of some of his predictions a did the power of his words move the minds of the people to accept him. Only then were they persuaded that, indeed, *chisokoro* were truly speaking to them through him as a prophet. Little wonder then that some of his ideas remained in force long after his death.

Sakagwa in Old Age and Death

Even at his advanced age, Sakagwa continued to point fingers at the various Gusii clans and their hostilities against one another. He warned that the warring weakened them as a people. For example, he was distressed by the fights among the clans of MwaMosioma, MwaGichana, MwaMonari, MwaKibagendi, Abageka, Abagusero, and Abanchari, among others, which always had land disputes and came to him for advice.

It is said that he could, at times, refuse to listen to their complaints when he thought what they were doing was unreasonable. This disappointed those involved and made them hate him. Some started telling lies and strange stories about him and making evil plans against him.

These things made Sakagwa sad, his heart became heavier and troubled more than ever before. He became more and more stressed. When such things happened, he could consult *chisokoro* more often and more seriously than before. He could disappear from home for as long as three days without telling anybody anything regarding where he was. It was not uncommon for him, and those around him understood his conduct. All along, whenever he was confronted with a big issue, or whenever any leaders from any ethnic group or clan came to him with a serious problem or consultation, he would disappear into the forest or some strange place to speak to *chisokoro* who could guide him on the next course of action. The people understood that what he was doing was essential because of his role as a seer, counsellor and strategist, his age notwithstanding.

*****

Sakagwa must have felt and seen his death coming even as he continued serving the community.

It is told that, one time, he disappeared into the forest for three days. This was not unusual for those that were around him. It is what followed that confounded many.

After days of soul-searching and serious consultations with *chisokoro*, Sakagwa came back to his family. It is said that, this time, he was cheerful and more entertaining than he usually was. He was a changed person.

It is said that before he disappeared for the three days to consult *chisokoro*, he used to eat alone in his small house, *egesa*. However, once he came back from the forest, he was clearly transformed! He instructed that the family sit down to eat together. Henceforth, the whole family could sit together and share meals. At the time, his family consisted of Riogi, Nyamacharara, his second wife Kwamboka and her three children Nyamweno, Kemuma and Mogire.

One evening as they were having supper, Sakagwa told the family that he had an important message that he would pass to them soon. He warned them that the message would either be good or bad news to them.

The next day, the family, specifically his older sons Riogi and Nyamacharara, became anxious and implored the Mzee to deliver the message to them. It would appear that *chisokoro* had come to him in a dream and revealed to him that he was about to leave this world; he would join them, *chisokoro,* in the spiritual world in the very near future. He revealed this message to his family after their supper. He strongly warned them never to disclose it to anyone.

He added one more thing: that before his departure from this world, he had been advised to perform one major function. This was to host a big farewell party and invite all his friends, especially the leaders of all Gusii clans and the neighbouring communities.

The Farewell Party[2]

In preparation for the farewell party, Sakagwa sent emissaries and word all over Gusii and beyond to those he wanted to attend. At home, he provided directions on how the party would go, who would attend and even the schedule of events.

Eventually, the party was successfully held, with his plans and instructions followed to the letter.

On the material day, Sakagwa and his sons woke up at dawn and started preparations for the day. In the homestead, he had many domestic animals – cows, goats, sheep and countless chicken. According to the arrangements, the biggest and fattest bull[3] in the *boma* was slaughtered at dawn

---

2   The account of this party has a mix of details gleaned from community lore passed down generations as well as those capture in some of the references, notably Enock Matundura's *Sakagwa's Ghost*, as translated by Kefa Otiso, Nsemia Inc. 2020

3   **Editor's Note:** *Some accounts have it that in the Sakagwa lineage there was always a special bull,* eeri y'omochie, *which had been sired by another that came from generations of bulls in the family. It was the biggest bull in the home and it must have sired future bulls that*

and the cooking started in earnest. Several sheep, goats and chicken were also slaughtered as the day progressed. By midmorning the guests had arrived in their numbers and the party started with the drinking of the local brew which was supplied in plenty.

The guests came from all corners – Luoland, Maasailand, Kurialand, Kipsigis and of course Gusii. By midday, guests were still arriving and the celebration continued. They included clan elders and other leaders.

Clan elder Angwenyi of Kitutu was designated as the chief organizer and master of ceremony at the event. According to the programme of the day, Angwenyi, assisted by Mzee Ogaro, opened the ceremony with greetings and a few welcoming remarks.

First, he informed the guests that the party was being hosted by prophet Sakagwa. He informed the guests that the ceremony was to start with some entertainment. However, before the entertainment, Sakagwa was invited to greet the gathering and formally welcome them to his home. The guests were mainly seated under the big tree in his compound (*omogoroka o'Sakagwa*). It was under this tree where Sakagwa normally sat to receive guests, those coming from within and outside of Gusii. It is also under this tree that he pronounced most of his prophecies and dispensed medicine, including *ebiranya*.

It is reported that Sakagwa's address was brief and prophetic. He welcomed everybody and thanked all the guests for coming to the party. He informed all and sundry that there was plenty

would take its place; it could only be slaughtered if it already had progeny to assure continuity.

Sample plant similar to Omogoroka o'Sakagwa

to eat and drink. The purpose of the party was to thank God, *Engoro,* and the ancestors (*chisokoro*) for the opportunity they gave him to serve the people and transform the society, especially the Gusii community where he belonged. He told them that there was entertainment to grace the ceremony, which was officiated by Mzee Ogaro.

Entertainment followed soon after his speech.

First, it was the young Gusii warriors who took the stage and entertained the guests with their skills on how to protect the home and the community at large. Besides protection for the community, they displayed their skills and techniques on providing security for themselves, their families and the wider societies. They were led through all these activities by their leader. Before leaving the stage, they announced that their presence during this ceremony was, besides entertainment, to also provide security and deal with any cases of hooliganism during the ceremony. They then displayed to the guests the different weapons at their disposal. They explained how, when and what the weapons – spears, clubs, arrows, shields and sling shots - were used for.

Next on the stage were middle-aged young men who played *obokano* (the harp, lyre) in turns. Some beat drums while the others danced to the tune of the sweet music. The young men were dressed in their traditional attire. They received a standing ovation from the crowd.

The ladies did not miss out on the occasion. They took the stage in their traditional regalia and entertained the guests, with various types of dances including those that are given during special occasions like *ribina* and others.

As well, old men danced in style and sang Gusii traditional songs (including *emeino*) that were relevant to the occasion.

To crown the entertainment, younger men took the stage and performed activities like dancing, wrestling and boxing, all with a traditional touch. They were all dressed in the best traditional wear possible. The entertainment ended with a light touch of the young men's traditional dancing, somersaulting and acrobatics.

The climax came up at around dusk. Still, there was plenty of food. All the guests including children and everybody ate as much as their stomachs could hold.

As evening approached, guests who came from far showed intentions to leave. But just before they could, do so, Elder Angwenyi took to the stage and made some remarks. He thanked all the guests for coming in large numbers and for being orderly.

Finally, Elder Angwenyi thanked Sakagwa's family. He gave special thanks to Mzee Sakagwa for the colourful ceremony and the hospitality. He then invited other elders from outside Gusii to give a few remarks. When they were done, he invited the host to close the ceremony.

Sakagwa reiterated that he had purposely staged the event as a farewell party to thank *Engoro* and *chisokoro* for the chance they gave him to serve the people. He singled out uniting Abagusii and bringing about sustainable peace.

His farewell speech was brief and to the point, but it ended on a sad note. He surprised everybody when he announced that this party marked the end of his prophecies. Henceforth, he declared, he would not be practising any activities of his occupation as a seer and that all his paraphernalia had been returned to his ancestors. The announcement left everybody in great shock and disbelief.

Soon the party came to a close and everyone dispersed to go to their homes.

Controversial Death, Burial & Dismay

It was in December of the year 1902, when Sakagwa died under very bizarre circumstances. Just the previous day, he had hosted a multitude of guests at his Gesoni home. It was a big party, attended not only by Gusii leaders, but also others from the surrounding communities – the Luo, the Maasai, Kuria and the Kipsigis.

It was a major consternation to the community to hear about the seer's death so soon after the party. To this day, Sakagwa's death remains as mysterious as his life was. There are three major theories on how he died and present them here accordingly.

The narratives given in this part give the story about the demise and burial of a great Gusii prophet, Sakagwa, son of Ng'iti are as told by different people, including one version by the family. Our different informants hardly knew who Sakagwa was, but said that they understood that he was a great man of influence of his time, and a prophet of the people of Gusii.

Given the passage of time and the inevitable 'distortion' that comes with telling and retelling a story, the versions differ. More so, they also differ because of the version told is dependent on what was originally passed down and by whom.

In this scenario, it is not surprising to find some informants telling us that surely Sakagwa did not die – he could not have died, because the people wanted him to come back as a saviour.

Here we offer four versions that we came across; three of them are simple variations of each other while the fourth one came from members of the family.

Theory One

One theory explains that Sakagwa threw a farewell party for his friends. Just before the friends arrived, he and his sons brought the biggest bull from the herd; they slaughtered the bull, without skinning it. They then cut the head, the hooves and the legs and left it bulging just outside the house. When the guests came, they were told that Sakagwa was sick in the house. On their request to see him, they were allowed to enter and see him but to their surprise, they were shown a 'heap' covered with hides and they were told that that was Sakagwa in deep sleep.

They were not allowed to wake him up, so they reluctantly returned to their homes without seeing him.

Soon after that, they heard that Sakagwa was dead! They immediately rushed to his home and found many people who had come to mourn him. Strange as it was, all the people were turned away by family members. They were simply told that Sakagwa had died and there was to be no mourning in the home. They went back to their homes in great shock!

After two days, Elder Angwenyi and other friends of Sakagwa came to Sakagwa's home and demanded an explanation about the death. They were not given any and so they requested to exhume the body. They were allowed to do so. Some strong young men immediately embarked on the work. It was a shallow grave and, after a short while, they found the head of the bull that had been slaughtered for the party, his stool and walking stick. Sakagwa's body was nowhere in the grave. The onlookers and the youth involved in digging up the grave were in great shock! They left the grave open and everybody fled to their homes in utter shock and disbelief.

> **Editor's Note:** *that Sakagwa held a farewell party is entrenched in the understanding of the seer's last days alive. The notion that his guests never saw him suggests some distortion. As such, it is possible that this version of the story was conjured up by someone who was not close to the events of the time. The story could be plausible to those that revered the prophet and hence believed in the mystery surrounding this version of the story of Sakagwa's death.*

Theory Two

Another narrative about Sakagwa's death and burial is told as follows: when Sakagwa had become very old, he called his friends and many other people for a cerebration. The celebration would take place in midmorning at his homestead. Sakagwa was to slaughter one of the fattest bulls he had in his herd.

On the material day of the celebration, the story goes, Sakagwa woke up very early and, with his sons, slaughtered the bull before everybody had arrived. Then, he took his four-legged stool, and the bull's head and tail. He then proceeded to the middle of his homestead where he put the bull's head and tail under his stool and sat down. He then sunk slowly and disappeared as everyone present watched.

The narrative then says that, when the people who had not reached Sakagwa's home in time were told about this, they did not believe it. At his homestead, they demanded proof of Sakagwa's death and burial. However, when nobody came up to give them an explanation, they decided to dig up the spot of Sakagwa's grave. First, they found the four-legged stool, his walking stick, then the bull's head and the tail. Sakagwa's body was not in the grave. People present got very scared and everybody ran away in great panic.

> **Editor's Note:** *as with the first narrative, this version fails to acknowledge that the farewell party happened and that it is only after the party that the shocking news of the seer's death came. It is possible that, as with the first narrative, that the original version was conjured up by people that were not close to the events of the day and place.*

As well, it could also be plausible given the seer's status in society and the mysteries surrounding his life.

Theory Three

The third version is perhaps the most widely held theory of the death of the sage. It mixes both mystery and disbelief, except for failure to locate the seer's body in the grave.

This version of the story holds that, indeed, Sakagwa called and held a big party in his homestead that was attended by many from within and outside the Gusii community. The party was a success and guests feasted, fed well by the sumptuous meals and drinks offered. Indeed, this version holds, Sakagwa did slaughter the fattest bull in the homestead, several goats, sheep and chicken.

Strange things started in the night following the dispersal of guests. It is said that people heard wailing from Sakagwa's home and wondered what could have happened. They soon found their way there and were shown his freshly covered grave outside the house.

Pandemonium soon broke as many more people came to find out what happened, many of them in sombre mood and others mourning and wailing loudly for having lost such a famous man; and more so because they had left on a jolly mood following the party.

As the day progressed, this version goes, elders started questioning the wisdom of burying such a prominent person so quickly after his death. Why couldn't the family wait? They wondered! How come not one elder was invited to the burial? They asked! And, yes, more and more questions arose. The mystery deepened and the family could not offer a plausible explanation of what happened.

Finally, the elders decided to verify that Sakagwa had indeed died and was buried as the family said. They got some muscular young men to dig up the grave, only to find Sakagwa's stool, his walking stick, the head of the bull that had been slaughtered for the previous day's feast as well as the sage's flywhisk!

It was a shocker that sent many people fleeing the homestead!

This version holds that, with many speculating what may have actually happened, they would soon be convinced considering the sage's enigmatic life and words at the party. So, even as they wondered what happened, they reluctantly accepted that the prophet's mysterious powers must have been at work. That 'reality' stood unchallenged and remains so, for many, to date.

Editor's Note: *given Sakagwa's mysterious personality, his knowledge of medicines, his apparent prophecies and the like, there is no wonder that this version has remained predominant for a long, long time. One can remotely relate to the 'rise' of Jesus where his family comes to his tomb and not find the body of Jesus. They ended up believing, and passing this it down generations that Jesus indeed rose and went to heaven. Abagusii of the time must have believed that the lack of Sakagwa's body could be ascribed to his mysterious powers. Would chisokoro have been responsible for this mystery? They wondered!*

The Family Version

One theory concerning his death, which is not widespread but is acceptable in the community among those who have come across it, is that immediately after the farewell party, which ended around midnight, Sakagwa summoned his family and explained to them as to why he had hosted the party. He told them that *chisokoro* had called him to join them in the ancestral world. He gave them clear instructions regarding his burial and strong warnings about revealing the details.

They were to dig two graves – one for him and another one for his personal items. The grave for his personal items was to be dug outside the main house, in line with Abagusii customary law regarding burials. In this grave were to be buried his famous stool, which he always carried with him to all clan or tribal councils, his walking stick and flywhisk. The head of the bull which he had slaughtered for his guests the previous evening was also to be buried in the same grave.

The grave where his body would be laid to rest was to be dug inside the main house. It is said that Sakagwa himself dug and prepared this grave according to his design. He was assisted by his two sons, Riogi and Nyamacharara and the bottom of the grave was prepared like a bed. Sakagwa reportedly selected the personal items which he arranged inside the grave – his personal attire, some of his paraphernalia and gourd full of milk. He told the family that he needed to carry these in his journey to the world of the ancestors.

When he was satisfied with all the preparations, the story goes, Sakagwa sat with his two sons and wife and gave them thorough, specific and confidential instructions. They were to bury him alive with the items the way he had arranged them. He warned them never to disclose to anybody that he had been buried at this spot in the house. Instead, they were to tell those inquiring that he had been buried in the grave outside the house. He further told them that, after a day or two, his *chisokoro* would come and take him to the ancestral world, but he would still be with them and would be protecting them from evils of every kind. He warned them over and over again that his burial was to be performed in utmost secrecy.

He had good reasons to do this. Specifically, even as many revered his place in the community, there were others who took a dim view of the prophet. Indeed, some people in the community and their leaders had become great enemies of Sakagwa because of his elevated place in the society, especially with respect to his prophecies, medicines, leadership and influence of most clan elders. He indicated that there were some that envied his position and could be plotting to kill him alongside his family. This was the reason he planned his burial to be carried out in high secrecy. According to his instructions, he was to be buried during the night, after which the personal items would be buried in the shallow grave outside.

The last instruction he gave was that the top of his grave (known as *ekebure* in Ekegusii) in the house was to be prepared and camouflaged. It was to be set to look like a fireplace, with fire and three cooking stones. This fire would be kept burning throughout as custom held whenever the family patriarch died.

In those days, respectable personalities (medicine men, prophets, outstanding warriors, foremost clan leaders and the like) were buried in a sitting position along with their belongings. The family says this is what happened with Skagwa's burial inside the house. As strange as that sounds, remember taht cultures, traditions, customs and norms are all transient and change from one generation to another and age to age, relative to circumstances prevailing at a particular time.

> **Editor's Note:** *in a conversation with Nemwel Atemba[4], who also gave the Ekegusii name (*ekebure*) for a grave that was inside the house, he indicated that the tradition of burying prominent people inside the house and in a sitting position was common among Abagusii and some Luhya subgroups, perhaps a mark of their common origins. The grave was prepared to be deep enough to accommodate the person in a sitting position; at the bottom of the grave was placed a big pot (*enseka*) in which the person sat and before filling the grave with soil the head was covered with a smaller pot (known as* egetono*). Clearly, given Sakagwa's prominence, it is interesting that none of the elders thought of the possibility of his body being buried inside the house. That said, it could also be due to his mysterious personality that such a thought never crossed anyone's mind.*

Sakagwa told his two sons and wife all the things that would happen after his death, but they were never to disclose anything to anybody.

All these activities of burial were accomplished before dawn. Then, the members of the family wailed and blew the horn as a sign that death

---

[4] Nemwel Atemba is the author of *Abagusii Wisdom Revisited* (Nsemia Inc., 2011), a collection of Ekegusii proverbs and their interpretation.

had struck the family. The whole of Bogeka clan was disturbed by the wailing and clan members rushed to seer's homestead and joined the family in weeping. By and large, the volume of the wailing increased and it pierced the still night of Gusii highlands.

On the new, yet sad, day, the whole of Gusii learnt of the death of prophet Sakagwa. By midmorning, it was impossible to find standing space in Sakagwa's homestead. Women in their thousands wept bitterly while men, who are traditionally expected to contain their pain and emotions during such occasions, visibly fought a losing battle against their unconquerable emotional pain and tears. Dogs barked in response to women's shrill voices. Even the cattle moved and behaved uncannily, according to community lore.

All this was attributed to Sakagwa's mystery, fame and greatness in Gusii.

The Luos, the Maasai and the Kipsigis also came in large numbers. Most of them were armed in case the people of Gusii turned hostile. They came, men and women, to pay their last respects to the great diviner and medicine man whose services knew no ethnic boundaries and whose medicine they had come to rely on.

When the wailing abated, elders pensively huddled at the centre of Sakagwa's homestead, beneath the large o*mogoroka* tree, under which the prophet used to receive his visitors. This matter had caused not only a great stir, but also irritation, among the people who seriously demanded a thorough explanation of the happenings. What was most utmost concern to them was that when the earliest mourners streamed into Sakagwa's

Sakagwa in Old Age and Death

home, they discovered that he had already been buried!

After serious discussions, the elders of Gusii, Luo, Kipsigis and Maasai pooh-poohed this action as embarrassingly foreign to known African traditions. They demanded a full account regarding Sakagwa's death and burial. So many questions were raised but there were no answers!

Meanwhile, Sakagwa's wife and children were not even around!

How could an elder and prophet of Sakagwa's stature be buried secretly in the night? How could a great elder and herbalist of Gusii be buried so hurriedly and without due ceremony and traditional funerary rituals? Who performed the burial ceremony? Who dug the grave? Was Sakagwa in that grave, which appeared so small?

Under the chairmanship of Elder Angwenyi, the elders unanimously resolved that Sakagwa's body be exhumed and reburied in a manner that would befit a person of his stature - an elder, medicine man and prophet. This decision was unanimously accepted and exhumation started immediately.

The mourners now waited in abated breath. It was such a shallow grave[5] that as soon as the exhumers started their work, they came across Sakagwa's famous stool; the one he used to carry with him to all clan or tribal councils. Further digging revealed his walking stick and fly whisk. As they dug deeper, they found the head of the bull which had been slaughtered for his guests the previous day.

5 It is noted that Sakagwa's homestead stood at Gesoni a rocky hill that would have been very difficult to crack and hence the shallowness of the 'grave'.

But alas! The prophet's body was nowhere to be found!

So shocked were the mourners that wailing stopped. This was yet another mysterious episode in the life of Sakagwa. Many mourners, uncertain of how to respond to the situation, disappeared in panic. Others, dumbfounded, remained dreadfully confused about the death and burial. They were left with very many questions unanswered.

However, those who had previously followed Sakagwa's behaviour and activities, especially the activities of the previous day, argued that it was possible that Sakagwa had died and that either he moved into the netherworld or *chisokoro* might have come and simply taken away his body!

Fear and despondence engulfed Sakagwa's home, the Bogeka clan and the neighbouring villages with others speculating that Sakagwa would return soon with his ancestors to take firm control of the body. Sakagwa's family and the whole of Gesoni area lived in great fear for many days.

*****

When all was said and done, the life and character of Sakagwa were such that the mysterious circumstances surrounding his death were soon accepted as possible. Sakagwa is remembered among Abagusii as a thoroughly mysterious man. He was capable of miraculously appearing and disappearing in many occasions, they reasoned. Some claimed that, at times, he could transform himself into different persons, or into beasts, to impress or confuse his adversaries. Sakagwa's legend was that he occasionally went away, appeared and disappeared. As such, anything that could be imagined was possible.

Sakagwa in Old Age and Death

The belief grew stronger that Sakagwa would suddenly come back to earth again to continue with his prophecies. After some time, there were stories that he had been seen at several places, wearing a simple leather garment and a rough goat-hair cloak of a country man. He was always bare foot and had a long flowing beard, some claimed. On several occasions, it was said, young girls who went to the river in the neighbourhood to fetch water saw a person seated on a big stone which was by the side of the river. The girls would be so scared that they would run back to their homes and report the unusual occurrences to their parents. When the parents would come to see this strange person, they could not see any. This happened several times and over many years, and the elders concluded it was Sakagwa's ghost.

As unbelievable as it may sound, there are many other theories and stories about Sakagwa's death and burial.

> **Editor's Note:** *this version was provided by living members of the family of Sakagwa. Over generations, they passed it down within the family but none dared share it with the rest of the world as they too feared meeting the repercussions the seer had warned about. Having said that, and as unbelievable as it may sound, there are many other theories and stories about Sakagwa's death and burial, most of them that have morphed with decades upon decades of telling and retelling. for example, there are other that claim that Sakagwa 'sneaked' into the land of the Kipsigis where he settled and started a family, which of course if not true. Yet many entertain that possibility.*

Why Sakagwa's Death & Burial Confound Many

Based on the foregoing discussion, it is no wonder that Sakagwa's demise and burial remain a mystery to this day. The differing accounts explaining his death and burial are by no means an accident and could, perhaps, be the way the seer had intended.

Recall that when the exhumers failed to find Sakagwa's body in the grave most of the mourners were awe-stricken and many fled in panic.

What happened to the grave that had been totally opened but was empty? This is one of those questions that will remain unanswered for a long time. There has been little account of this with more focus laid on the mysterious death.

When Elder Angwenyi, who was the master of ceremony during the farewell party and the overseer of the exhumation exercise, was asked this question after some time, he could not remember what happened. However, members of Sakagwa's family recalled later in life that the grave was refilled the next day and remained guarded, apparently according to the departed patriarch's instructions. As it was later learnt, there were certain secrets which Sakagwa left only with his wife and the two older sons. It would appear that details about his grave are some of the secrets that the family needed to keep to the end.

Remember that, according to family accounts, there were two graves: one inside the house and another one outside. Sakagwa was buried in the grave in house. As such, for all intents and purposes, this should be regarded as Sakagwa's grave, to this day. The grave that was dug outside was used as a camouflage for security reasons, known to the seer and his family.

Sakagwa's 'grave' on the outside remained a very significant spot in the homestead as is the case with most African communities. Having been regarded as the most famous prophet in Gusii, and considering the circumstances under which he died and was buried, this grave was feared and respected almost in equal measure. Nobody could dare step near it for fear of being attacked or cursed by *chisokoro*.

It is said that, a few days after the burial, a big mound was built on the grave. Some herbal trees were planted around it. With time, a mound 'grew' from underneath. As a sign of honour and respect, the family erected a small fence around the grave. A special tree grew right at the centre of the grave and became quite big over the years. It came to be known as *Omogoroka o'Sakagwa*, and became a new landmark similar to the one under which he held court. It was the same tree species that Sakagwa kept in his compound, under which he used to receive his visitors.

As years went by, stories sprung in all sorts of places that Sakagwa's ghost could be seen on this grave on many days, especially around midnight. Also, there were claims that every evening at the grave, there could be seen a fire and some smoke. Strangely, however, according to the claims, when one approached the site, one saw nothing. With the fire and smoke, could also be heard sounds of crocking frogs but as one approached, everything went silent and disappeared completely, the tales went.

More strange happenings kept being reported about the grave.

Even in recent times, as late as 2007, a group of about ten women who were digging, like they always did, received a shock of their lives! They were in their traditional self-help group (*egesangio*) one midmorning and digging. It was a fine morning and the sun was shining brightly. It happened that they were digging together at the *shamba* where Sakagwa was buried, near his grave. Out of curiosity, some of the women dug very close to the grave, removing some parts covering the grave. These women knew very well that Sakagwa's grave was a sacred spot, but they deliberately dug as close to the grave as they could – only to get a shock of their lives!

It was reported that, in broad day light, when the sun was shining very brightly and there wasn't even a single cloud in the sky, just from nowhere, there came a loud thunderstorm, which enveloped the group of women only. The women were struck and they all fell on the ground facing different directions. It took a fair amount of time for them to regain their consciousness. Soon, each one of them fled from the scene, leaving behind all items, including their *jembes*. Also, after this thunderstorm, a big crack occurred at this part of the grave. The crack remained visible for many years.

Sakagwa in Old Age and Death

THE CUCTUS TREE THAT GREW ON PROPHET SAKAWA'S GRAVE

THE HEAP OF STONES SHOW PROPHET SAKAWA'S GRAVE

Aftermath of Sakagwa's Death

In his life, Sakagwa rose to play the role of a leader in many respects and especially a spiritual leader of Abagusii. As an intercessor between the living and *chisokoro*, this important role served the community's spiritual needs. It is no wonder, therefore, that once he died the community experienced a vacuum. With his death, no one appeared to rise to 'fit into his shoes' that now appeared too large to fill.

Nature avers a vacuum and hence there emerged other forms of spiritual inclinations that were modulated by protest due to the subjugation occasioned by entrenchment of colonial domination.

Mumboism[6]

Following the death of Sakagwa and the spiritual vacuum[7] he left, there emerged in Gusii a movement that came to be known as *Enyamumbo* or *Mumboism* as some historians refer to it. It had origins in Luoland and, at the centre of it, was by

---

6 A lot of content in this section relies on publications by W. R. Ochieng and J. S. Akama which we found as ample sources of information; here we have contextualized the historical phenomenon and the relationship with the spiritual gap left due to Sakagwa's death.

7 **Editor's Note:** *Many historians such as W. R. Ochieng', B. A. Ogot and Robert Maxon have analyzed Mumboism as a political movement where religion was used as a 'cover'. While that may be so, our argument is that in Gusii, the movement found fertile ground in part due to the spiritual vacuum that came with the death of Sakagwa. That said, there is no doubt that it was an anti-colonial movement.*

the name of Onyango Dunde. Reportedly, it had many followers around Lake Victoria.

Onyango Dunde, it is said, preached that he had been chosen by God (Mumbo) to rescue them from European subjugation. He urged them to shun European culture which he condemned vehemently alongside Christianity and colonialism. Dunde further preached that, very soon, a golden age would arrive, which would end the European presence in Nyanza region. As it spread from Alego to Central Nyanza and other places, Mumboism had the makings of a protest movement, rebelling against foreign influences and domination.

According to tales, Onyango Dunde and Mori Auma, the Mumbo proponents, preached that they had met and talked to Mumbo, who had promised them that all Mumboists would get free food from heaven and there was no need for them to till their land or plant any crops. The followers were also informed that the non-Mumboists would experience terrible life on earth – for instance, they would have no food from their *shambas* and in their homes; water would turn into blood and only Mumboists would have clean drinking water.

Soon, word got to Gusii and some people from the region made their way to Alego to study this movement and to understand what it was all about. It appears that, with the spiritual vacuum Sakagwa left and having died without a designated successor, his adherents went around searching for alternatives and hence the latch towards Mumboism.

On their return, they introduced the Mumboist beliefs among their clans. Here, they found fertile ground as many people in Gusii at the time were already disappointed with the British influence. Followers of Mumboism were made to believe that they had become God's chosen people, and that they should all acknowledge Him forever. This way, they hoped that they will always live in peace and have plenty forever. It was imparted on Mumboists that Christianity, which the Europeans had introduced, was a rotten religion through which white people enslaved Africans. As such, Africans needed to stand firm and fight European domination with all their might in defence of their land and other possessions[8].

Adherents wore white goat skins and expressed their distaste for European ways by allowing their hair to grow long. They also smoked bhang.

The advent of Mumboism rekindled Sakagwa's prophecy of an end to European colonialism which he had preached to Abagusii. The result was an open revolt against European colonialism in years of 1905, 1908 and 1914.

> **Editor's Note:** *The years coincided with major milestones in the establishment of colonial rule in Gusii. 1905 represented the first incursion into Gusii where there was fierce resistance despite many losses of warriors. The resistance caused the colonizers to pull back for reinforcement and came back in full force in 1907/08 to subdue the opposition which they succeeded in doing with the surrender of Otenyo Nyamaterere. The year 1914 represents the breakout of the World War I when German soldiers temporarily overran the British*

---

8 **Editor's Note:** *According to Z. O. Ogamba Enyamumbo was indeed a protest movement and that practitioners congregated as if they were praying. In reality they were plotting their resistance against the colonialism of the white man. They rejected the white man's religion, his administration and his goods.*

> *stronghold in present-day Kisii Town. During this time, Abagusii sided with the Germans who they saw as saviours from the brutal British domination. When the war turned around, however, and the Germans were ferreted out of Gusii, the British took a major revenge against Abagusii that saw hundreds of Abagusii dead as the colonialists re-established themselves in Gusii.*

Many people from Kitutu welcomed the Mumbo movement, where clan Elder (later called chief) Nyakundi was already preaching against the British.

Mumboism first entrenched itself in Wanjare led by Twara and Omwenga. From Wanjare it spread to Kitutu and was embraced by Elder Nyakundi together with Ogworo. Soon it spread to North Mugirango and Nyaribari, with leaders like Mochoronge and Ondieki, respectively.

The Mumboist movement was overshadowed by the breakout of World War I, 1914 – 1918, that pitted the British and Germans in Gusii. Here German soldiers overran and took over the British establishment in Kisii Town. As it turned out, the German forces overpowered the British and they forced their way into Kisii Town, Boma. A lot of looting took place in the town and the mission stations around it.

The British later turned tables and forced the Germans to withdraw as fortunes turned around. When the British retook Kisii Town, they attacked the rebellious Abagusii and confiscated large herds of cattle. Many young Gusii warriors were conscripted into the Carrier Corps while others were sent out of the district to work in Europeans plantations. Clearly, this was British revenge against Abagusii for what was seen as the latter's tacit support for the now routed German soldiers.

By 1919, Mumboism had become a politically subversive force in Gusii, although the colonial Government did not appear to fully appreciate its potency. In 1919 when Mr. John Ainsworth, the Native Commissioner, was asked to shed more light on Mumboism, he gave the following personal views:-

> "I have personally known of this so-called religion for some years now but have not been of the opinion that it had any political significance, nor that it need to be interfered with. I think you (provincial commissioner) in Kisumu will agree that any needless interference with such matters is generally liable to make them stronger and also cause them to become more secretive and therefore possibly dangerous." - see W. R. Ochieng' in *Mumboism – An Anti-Colonial Movement.* 1969

*****

Between 1918 and 1919, a big famine ravaged most of western Kenya, including the lake region. The impact of the famine was worsened by the lack of food in many homes, courtesy of the teachings of the Mumbo preachers. Reportedly, these spiritualists had promised their followers that they would get free food from heaven, provided the adherents showed faith and remained steadfast in the 'religion'. Devotees now faced a shock of their lives!

With no food coming from either their *shambas* or heaven, many Mumboists died during this time. As the effects of the famine worsened across western Kenya, many of the sect's believers started to question the very premise and meaning of Mumboism. Where was this Mumbo when all his followers were suffering while some were dying? They asked. Where was this god Mumbo living when his people endured the kind of suffering they faced? They wondered.

Followers, especially those in Gusii, had been told that Mumbo (God) had talked with some Luo prophets like Onyango Dunde and Mori Auma. However, they now asked who amongst Abagusii had met and talked to Mumbo?

Having failed to get clear answers to these questions, nearly all the Gusii Mumboists became so disillusioned that they gradually drifted away to something else. They wanted to survive and Mumbo was not helping them in their struggles.

In Gusii, the Mwabogonko of the Kitutu Subclan, which was the wealthiest and most influential in the larger community and had strong adherents and leaders of Mumboism, was the last to abandon the cult. By that time the colonial Government felt quite threatened by the most fanatical Mumboists, who did their best to create fear among the people. They would cunningly, and even forcefully, solicit for donations of food and live animals from people's homes – under the pretext that these gifts were to be given to Mumbo to feed on.

Sakagwaism[9]

As indicated in the previous section, many Abagusii's dalliance with Mumboism ended in disappointment. They had failed to fathom the

---

9 Some spell this as Sakawaism; however, given we have adopted the correct version of the name Sakagwa, it is pertinent that we maintain that nomenclature and hence the name Sakagwaism.

sense and purpose of Mumboism from a spiritual angle. Left with neither spiritual direction nor beacon for navigation, they faced substantial soul-searching.

It is through this that a spiritual movement, which they finally understood, emerged. Fortunately for Abagusii, the new spiritual order shared many doctrinal elements in common with Mumboism.

This new movement was based on the teachings of Sakagwa. It is said that the movement was started by a woman named Bonareri (see Ochieng – *A Modern History of Kenya 1895-1980*).

Sakagwaism relied heavily on Sakagwa's prophecy that the white men would come to Gusii. As well, Sakagwa had warned the people of Gusii never to lift a finger against these intruders because they were to stay for a short while and go back to their country. Evidently, Abagusii tried twice to repulse the colonizers (in 1905 and 1908) with disastrous results. Based on these losses, a strong myth began to spread among Abagusii. It was said that Sakagwa, who had died in 1902, was the one who had brought the white people and was the only person who could remove them on his return.

Sakagwaism started in Kitutu and spread at a rapid rate to other parts of Gusii. Around the same time, the founder of Sakagwaism, prophetess Bonareri, setup a school to preach her brand of the new spiritual movement. However, the colonial government considered her mentally disturbed and threw her into a lunatic asylum at Kisii Town, Boma. She was later released and given a harsh warning against pursuing her activities. She went quiet thereafter.

Despite her going quiet, it appears that it became an opportunity for reflection as she would soon revisit her mission. As such, towards the end of 1920, she gathered a significant following whom she began to prepare for the arrival of Sakagwa, more like the Biblical second coming of Jesus. According to her, Sakagwa's return would completely remove the white man from Gusii. Using her sorceries and spiritual urge, she preached that on Sakagwa's arrival, there would be a plague of locusts. This would be followed by many days of total darkness, after which the white man would be no more.

Bonareri further 'prophesied' that Sakagwa would be a high priest and she (Bonareri) would be the prophetess, and the two would occupy *Getembe kia Gasuku* (Kisii Town). The two leaders would then ensure that the white man would never set foot in Gusii again.

By 1921, Sakagwaism had gained a staggering following across Gusii. The colonial government got alarmed that surely Sakagwa would arrive in a short while. The government closed Bonareri's school in a huff. Bonareri and her adherents were rounded up and put into prison.

It is worth noting that even as Sakagwaism took root, there were remnants of Mumboism in Gusii. Both movements continued to exist, albeit secretly, and in the year 1934, ten most fervent Mumboists were arrested and arraigned in a court in Kisii. They were sentenced and exiled to Kipini in Lamu Island on the Indian Ocean. The ten were:

1) Okenyuri
2) Omwenga
3) Nyakundi
4) Mori Auma
5) Onyango Dunde
6) Ontori
7) Mogaka
8) Mochingori
9) Nyamacharara
10) Onkomba

Mumboism and Sakagwaism became deep rooted in Gusii and lasted for a long while. This was against the wishes of the colonial government which found it a challenge to stamp out either of them completely. It appears that, even with government attempt to crash the movements, followers continued with their activities, albeit at a slower pace than before. And the two appear to have survived hand in hand. Finally in 1954, in the midst of the state of emergency declared in Kenya, the colonial government proscribed the two movements.

Sakagwa's Family after His Death

Sakagwa's death disrupted life for his family. Following the burial of the sage, the family found life unbearable at Gesoni. According to stories passed down generations, they constantly felt haunted by his ghost and *chisokoro*. These tribulations may suggest that Sakagwa's ghost and the *chisokoro* were in full control of the home, acccording to stories passed down generations.

By that time his sons, Riogi and Nyamacharara from the first wife Kerubo, were grown up men. On the other hand, as was the tradition then, the daughters Obare and Kemunto had been married off and had their own homes.

The sons wanted to marry and start their own families. However, the environment at Gesoni was not conducive for them. Few parents would accept their daughters to be married into homes that appeared tormented as Sakagwa's was. Aside from tribulations brought about by the death of the sage, the land they occupied was rocky and no meaningful farming could be done on it. The place, as discussed elsewhere, was aptly known as 'Getare', meaning rocky.

That said, the family, perhaps due to Sakagwa's instructions, braved the hardships and what came with it. They lived in a state of agony for long. However, when they could take it no more, and perhaps because their survival was at stake, they decided to migrate, specifically to look for land that was more arable and which could provide needed livelihood.

Sakagwa's Family After His Death

Once a decision was reached, Sakagwa's wife Kwamboka, her three sons and daughter, together with Riogi and Nyamacharara, migrated from the Gesoni home. At the time, there was a lot of free land everywhere and anybody could settle wherever they wanted. They moved and settled at Nyarenda, near Nyakoe - some three kilometers or so from Gesoni. Here, the land was fertile and the environment more friendly than at Gesoni.

*****

As was the tradition of the day, roles like the one Sakagwa held were passed down along families through generations. Sakagwa had inherited his art from his father and he too was obligated to pass it down to the next generation through one of his sons. For this, he had identified his first son Riogi as the heir to his trade of herbal medicine and other related activities. Accordingly, Riogi became the heir following his father's death.

Riogi practised the trade as he had learnt from his father, as directed and expected and as tradition held. Over time, his family grew, having married six wives.

As with his father, Riogi continued to learn and conduct the practice of herbal medicine as expected. He tried his best to do everything the way his father used to do. However much he tried, though, he could not measure up to his father's standards and stature . Furthermore, his eyesight began to fail him at a fairly early age and this had an impact on what he did and how well he did it. His treatments became less and less effective, perhaps because he could not accurately locate the specific plants meant for specific illnesses.

Faced with these unfortunate circumstances, Riogi and his first wife, Moraa, considered training one of their children to inherit the trade as tradition held. They settled on Moraa's fist-born son whom they had named Sakagwa[1] after the departed prophet.

Recall that, throughout Gusii and its environs, Sakagwa was known not only as a prophet but he was also a rainmaker, a magician, a strategist, a community wise man and the like. From this point of view it was prudent that these powers run down in the family of Sakagwa through inheritance, as was the practice. Indeed, had that happened, we would have someone in the lineage practicing the trade of herbal medicine, even at this point in time.

That was not to be! Why? It did not happen, because of rivalries inherent in large, and especially, polygamous homes.

It is said that Riogi and his first wife Moraa planned well to pass on the art to Moraa's son Sakagwa. The young man would inherit the tradition to become a traditional healer with Riogi's blessings.

Everything was set to happen as planned. However, Kibai, Riogi's third wife, who was known to be shy but sly, learnt about the plan before it was executed. She wanted the inheritance for her son Nyakundi.

---

1 **Editor's Note**: *in Gusii it was the practice to name children after people that had died. It was believed that, in doing so, the new born would take the good characteristics of the person after whom they were named. Indeed, some believed that the child would be the good person being reborn. Good people got many children named after them while hardly any children were named after individuals of poor reputation.*

Working with Nyakundi, she planned and stole Riogi's paraphernalia which used to be hidden secretly in a container in the granary outside the main house. One of the secrets about the paraphernalia was that it was never kept in the house. Practitioners believed that keeping it in the house made it lose its potency.

Unfortunately Kibai and her son were not privy to this secret detail which was kept secret except for those appointed to handle the paraphernalia. After stealing the paraphernalia, and happy that her son would be the heir to the practice, Kibai took it and hid it inside her house, in the ceiling-like storage space (*irongo*) that was part of traditional houses.

Kibai's next plan was to approach Riogi with her son to talk and convince him to accept to make Nyakundi the heir to the family's practice passed down generations.

However, that was not to be!

On the day of the planned meeting with Riogi about this fraudulent plan, a serious incident occurred in the home. It is said that, around midday and with nearly all the family in the homestead, everything seemed to be going on routinely. The women were sitting outside their respective houses and all the children were playing all over the compound. Suddenly, they saw smoke coming from Kibai's house! The house was on fire! This was mysterious and the fire appeared to burn strongly as if fanned by something even if it was not windy on that day. Everybody in the compound ran around in confusion, wailing and yelling and completely unable to do much to quell the rage of the fire. The neighbours responded and came in in large numbers, forming a crowd in the process. They simply stood at a distance and watched helplessly. Mzee Riogi, who was also in the compound, was equally helpless. He simply watched as the house of his third wife went down into ashes. Everything in the house was destroyed, including the paraphernalia that Kibai had hidden in there. It was a blow to the family heritage and trade that had served so many in the community for generations.

After this tragic incident, Kibai disappeared from the home for three days, perhaps shocked by the mystery of what had happened. It had long term consequences: the end of the spiritual, magical and seer activities of the family. No longer would this be passed to future generations!

*****

The acts of Kibai and her son bring to mind similar stories and especially those where mothers have planned to alter the path of designated inheritance, or the birthright blessings, of a particular child in favour of their preferences. A good example from the Bible, in the book of Genesis, is that of Rebecca and her favourite son Jacob, who planned and stole Esau's birthright. Working meticulous, they managed to dupe Isaac to believe that he was blessing Esau. It is also worthwhile noting that once such blessings have been given even to the unintended person, the act cannot be reversed. The same applies to curses: once pronounced, it is irrevocable. Indeed, most African communities believe that the blessing or a curse of a father or a mother is efficacious and permanent.

It is clear that Kibai knew this and wanted to ensure that Riogi would bless her son Nyakundi rather than Moraa's son, and the rightful heir, Sakagwa. She understood that once Riogi pronounced Nyakundi as the heir, the deal would be permanently sealed.

That said, many people believe that Kibai was punished for her errant act of wanting to subvert the appointed path of inheritance. This line of thought attributes the cause of the mysterious fire to the act of vengeful *chisokoro*.

*****

Stories passed down generations say that, after Sakagwa's family settled at Nyarenda, a mysterious fire started to be seen at night, some distance behind Riogi's house. It was similar to the fire that used to be seen near Sakagwa's house at Gesoni. Most people believe that it was the same fire that had 'followed' the family to Nyarenda, signifying a spiritual connection.

The fire at Nyarenda behind Riogi's house continued to burn for some years but also strangely wherever anybody approached the site nothing could be seen. It became extinct after Kibai's house burnt down. It would appear that this fire was tightly associated with Sakagwa and Riogi's paraphernalia. Once the artefacts went down in ashes, so also did the fire.

For believers, the way Kibai's house burnt down was a strong indication that *chisokoro* were not happy with her evil plan to steal the birthright blessings of another son. With her evil plan and act, it marked the end of Sakagwa's line of practice, including prophetic activities.

*****

Recent visits to Riogi's home at Nyarenda for oral interviews with Sakagwa's grandchildren is actually what revealed new information like what Kibai did. Joseph Nyakeindi, the only grandson of Sakagwa who is still alive, confirmed the story as captured in this book about his father Riogi and Sakagwa.

Nyakeindi confirmed that his father Riogi had six wives and that his mother Nyamokami was the fifth wife (*Nyageita*[2]) in line. From his mother, they were six sons and Nyakeindi was the fifth born. Riogi's sixth wife, added Nyakeindi, was called Boisabi. She was *omogomba*[3] and hence never bore any child.

Nyakeindi further remembers that his father used to stay alone in his hut. All the wives used to cook and bring food to the hut every evening. Inside the patriarch's hut every woman knew exactly where to place her share of the food. All the sons in the homestead would then sit around to eat with their father. However, before they started eating their father would examine and taste each of the dishes to ensure everything was properly done. And in case any of it was poorly cooked or was tasteless it could be taken back to the owner by the respective son. For the women, having one's food returned was some kind of

---

2 **Editor's Note:** Abagusii had a way they named their wives starting from number one to five, respectively, *Mobucha Ibu, Nyamesancho, Nyambweri Rogoro, Nyabweri Maate and Nyageita.* When a man married a sixth wife, the newly married woman went to live with the first wife; the seventh would go to live with the second wife and so on.
3 This is a term that refers to a woman who cannot bear children.

discipline as it was humiliating – here is a grown woman with children but who cannot cook!

Nyakeindi narrated that supper time was usually a very joyous time for the large family. It was the time their father told his sons interesting stories after which all the sons would disperse. The younger ones who had not been initiated would head to their respective mothers' houses while the older ones that had been initiated would go to the hut shared by all boys in the homestead.

Concerning the immediate family members, Nyakeindi vaguely remembers what their father told them. Riogi told his sons that Nyamacharara, their uncle, had moved from Nyarenda to settle near Nyakoe. With fading memory, Nyakeindi could not remember accurately where in the family tree to place names like Ng'iti and Nyakembugumbugu.

One other matter which he remembers vividly is that Riogi kept a bull that was very big and famous in the area. The bull was very wild and nobody could approach it except Mzee Riogi; only Riogi could feed it and give it directions. He recalled that the bull fought with and killed other bulls, something that happened on a number of occasions. For its size and strength, the bull became famous and many people travelled from far to see the animal. While it was known as Riogi's bull by many, it later acquired the nickname *Ongweso*. Also, the bull had another character according to Nyakeindi. It could wander far and wide, substantial distances away, but always came home at the end of the day.

During market days, at Nyakoe, Marani, Mosocho, Gesieka and other markets in the area, the bull could wake up in the early morning and go to these places. At the market, all the people knew Riogi's bull and its viciousness. As such whenever they saw it around, almost all of them fled away. Ongweso could then walk all over, eating what it could find until the stomach was full, after which it could walk home. Nyakeindi reported that Ongweso, Riogi's bull, lived to an old age.

Ongweso's end came with that of its owner! When Riogi died in 1952, and to offer a feast for mourners, Ongweso was cornered by group of many strong men, armed with axes, pangas, spears and all manner of crude weapons. It was overpowered and slaughtered.

Editor's Note: *as tradition held, many homes such as those of Sakagwa, kept a bull that was responsible for siring offspring with the cattle in the boma. This bull was specially bred and usually came from down the line of other bulls that had been with the family. Once a bull appeared that it was getting old, one of its offsprings could be reared to take its place. ... there is suspicion that Ongweso was a descendant of the bull that was slaughtered for the feat at Sakagwa's farewell party. If this is the case, then one can understand why the bull was treated in the manner it was treated.*

Sakagwa's Family After His Death

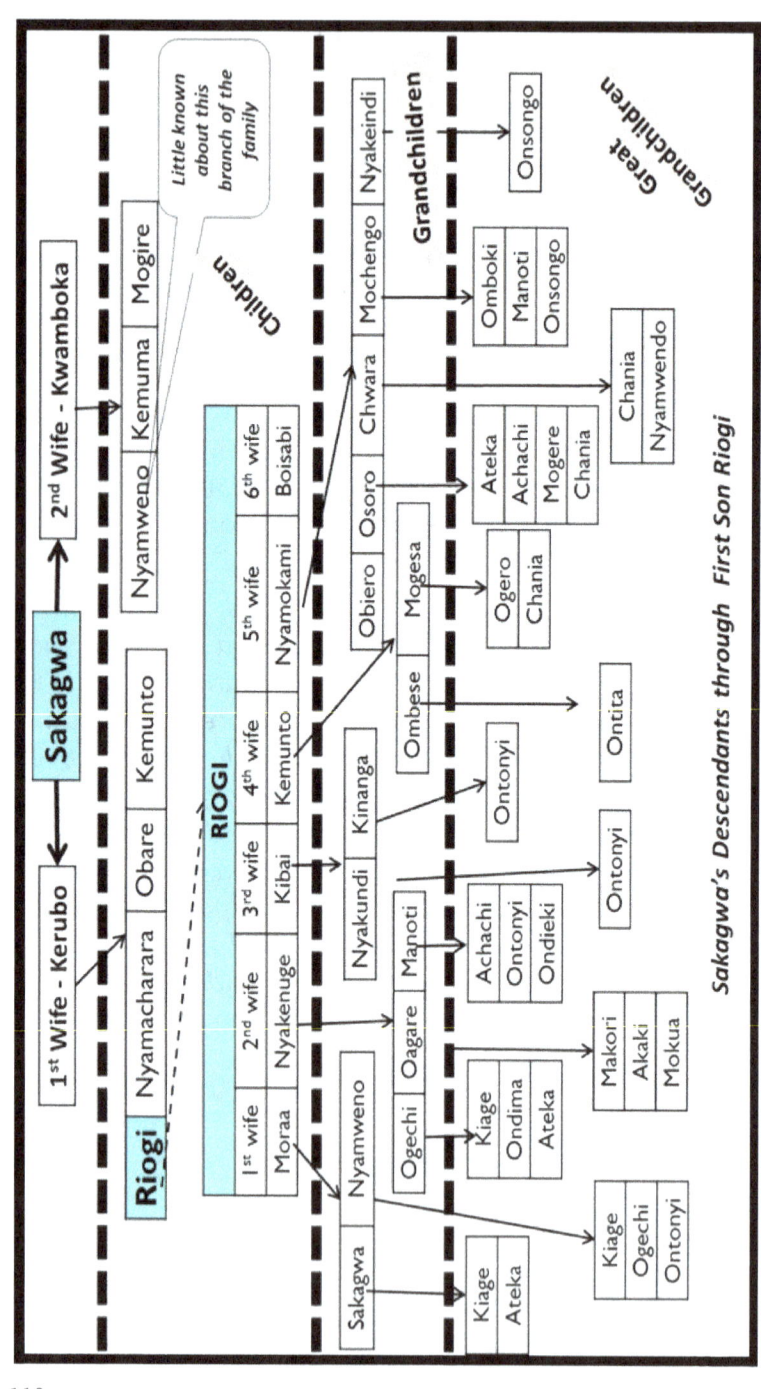

Sakagwa's Descendants through First Son Riogi

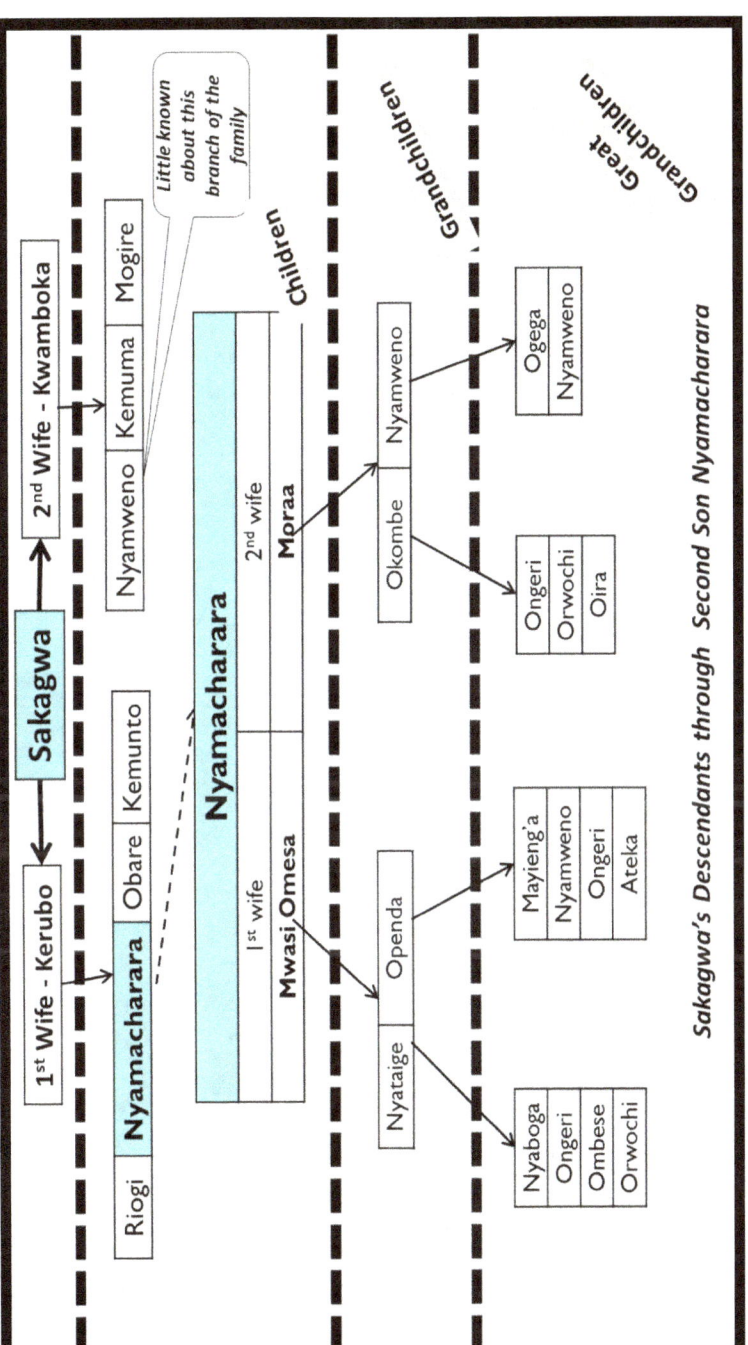

Sakagwa's Descendants through Second Son Nyamacharara

Joseph Nyakeindi (born around 1929) with his wife Margaret (2020)

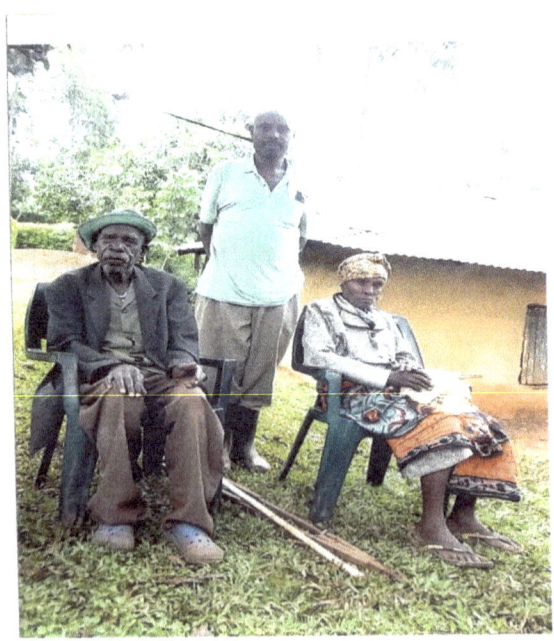

Joseph Nyakeindi (born around 1929) with his wife Margaret and a visitor from the community (2020)

The house of Joseph Nyakeindi and his wife Margaret Moraa

Sakagwa School & 'Shrine'

At this juncture the reader may be asking many questions. For example, what happened to the land at Gesoni where Sakagwa's homestead stood? How about his grave? Does it exist? This chapter attempts to answer some of these questions.

Sakagwa's Shrine

As discussed previously, Sakagwa's family moved to Nyarenda following the tribulations they faced at Gesoni following his death. After they abandoned the Gesoni home, the place remained deserted. It appears that nobody was interested in occupying the area due to fear of Sakagwa's ghost and the *chisokoro*. However, the people who knew Sakagwa and those who used to hear about him made frequent visits to the site, just to see the prophet's home and the grave.

These visits were, in part, triggered by curiosity because of stories that had spread, throughout Gusii, that Sakagwa's ghost was frequently sited on his grave especially around midnight. It was further claimed that, every evening, fire and smoke could be seen on the spot where he was buried. Strangely enough, the tales went, whenever somebody approached the site, everything disappeared.

With time, this place became a shrine of sorts in memory of the famous prophet.

We believe that it is with this consideration that, during the national land survey and demarcation process in mid 1960s, the area was set aside as public land. Measuring approximately two acres, the land was marked as Sakagwa's shrine. It remained so for all years.

Although the land exists, no formal shrine has been built for the famous prophet. It would be a great honour to have the place formally recognized as a heritage site and a shrine, properly curated and a fence erected in the place for protection. This would not only honour Sakagwa but also preserve the heritage for future generations.

Sakagwa School

The land of Sakagwa's homestead remained public land. Over time several efforts were made to put it in use for the good of the public. Those planning for the land never lost sight of the fact that they needed it to incorporate the memory of the great leader.

As such, in the 1980s and 1990s, some attempts were made by the community to start a nursery school on the land. The intentions hit a brick wall because the community lacked resources for the project. Also, there was no one willing to fund the project.

Separately, the Gusii County Council[4], in conjunction with the Ministry of Social Services, also made several attempts to build a monument for the prophet but this also never happened.

Around 2007, the community made another attempt to start a nursery school. This time the environment was favourable, what with

---

4 **Editor's Note:** *County Councils were part of the Local Government structure of the time; they handled issues like services (water, roads, school infrastructure and the like). They were scrapped and absorbed into the County Government structure following the promulgation of a new constitution in 2010.*

increasing population and pressure on existing school infrastructure. A number of parents saw the need for a school for their children since St. Peters Soko, the nearest one, is about 2 kilometres away. The parents came together and made contributions – especially in materials – to get the nursery started; some brought poles and rafters while others contributed old iron sheets. Still others brought whatever else they could manage. Having collected enough materials, in the spirit of *harambee*[5], they provided their own labour and put up two classrooms, for Nursery and Class One. They also employed a teacher who they paid directly.

At this time, St. Peters Soko had become congested due to introduction of free primary education. The school's Board of Management (BOM) was looking for ways to decongest the school. In their abundance outlook, the Sakagwa community together with the Soko Board of Management agreed to combine their efforts to address the issue. They built up Sakagwa School as a branch of St. Peters Soko. For purposes of convenience, this was a win-win for both sides since Sakagwa School had space to spare compared to St. Peters Soko and the two institutions were a short distance apart..

In 2009, the area MP, Hon. Richard Momoima Onyonka, came in to offer full-scale support for the school. Three permanent classrooms were constructed using money from the Constituency

---

5 The term *harambee* was popularized following the country's independence. It means 'to pull together' with each offering what they can and collectively making common tasks lighter.

Development Fund (CDF)[6]. Upon completion of the classrooms, many pupils from the neighbouring schools joined the up and coming school. In no time, the lower primary section was full to capacity.

The following year, 2010, Sakagwa School opened its doors and officially started its operations, with the Head Teacher, Deputy Head Teacher, some two teachers and a population of about 145 pupils. Gradually, more permanent classrooms were built with support from the CDF kitty under the patronage of the same MP. More children transferred from neighbouring schools and within a short while, nearly all the classes were full. With this rapid development, fuelled by modern infrastructure and devoted teachers, Sakagwa School attracted more and more children. This propelled it to a model school in the community. Today, the entire school is fully connected to electricity supply unlike some schools in the area.

In 2015, the school registered its first KCPE class, with 35 candidates. The results were impressive. It did much better than many schools in the Division. The Governor of Kisii, the Hon. James Omariba Ongwae, with the area Member of County Assembly (MCA) Hon Charles Mochoge Nyagoto and other guests visited the School in 2016, partly to see its progress and also see

---

6 The CDF is a nationally funded programme that was instituted in 2003 following the election of Mwai Kibaki to the presidency. It allocates money to go directly to constituencies to spend based on their priorities. It has brought impactful development at the grassroots where communities have put up schools, health clinics, rehabilitated water sources and paid fees for the needy, among others.

Sakagwa's grave. During the visit, the Governor expressed satisfaction with the school's progress and development. He donated some desks, chairs and tables for pupils and teachers, which the school urgently needed. Hon Nyagoto has also supported the school handsomely over time.

The school population has since grown and now stands at more than 600 pupils and 18 teachers posted by the Teachers' Service Commission.

Just outside the school compound there are Safaricom and Airtel communication masts which were installed even before the school was started. The installation of the masts near the school compound and the transformer for power supply have brought development to the surrounding community. Most homes around it have been connected to electricity in addition to getting good phone coverage.

To an extent, the establishment of Sakagwa School fulfils some of Sakagwa's prophecies, namely, that those parents who will manage to educate their children should never hesitate to do so because there will be plenty of opportunities at their door steps. In his words there will be plenty of 'mushrooms for harvesting'.

Inside the school compound, a big water tank has been constructed, part of Gesoni Water Project. The project, that is fully financed by the national government, was started in early 1980s and serves both Bogeka and Bogusero communities. The entire area around the school is fully connected to the Gesoni Water Supply. This gives the institution an advantage of getting the water even when there are no sufficient reserves for the entire area.

The Water Supply Project, the Kenya Power and Lighting transformer, the communications facilities and the school are all indicators of development and prestige in the community. They are symbols and indicators in any successful community in modern times. Modern life has changed how we live – we need piped water in our houses; we need electricity; we need better networks for our communication and better schools for quality education for our children. For the people around Sakagwa School, these prestige indicators have become part of their day to day way of life, as it were. The amenities have also become increasingly important for their psychological life as they feel to be part of the 'modern' world.

*****

Thinking in broader terms, the Bogeka community of the Gesoni or Sakagwa clan, where Sakagwa School has been built, there is great sense of belonging and pride of association to prophet Sakagwa. This is so because they accept him as a member of their community and feel proud of him as a key personality who had a major impact on the people of Gusii. They also see him as the man behind all the development in the area considering that the development has taken place courtesy of the name of Sakagwa.

More importantly, this brings us to the understanding of clan society. In such societies, what matters more than anything else to the individual members is that all should be accepted as members. They also have a recognized community to which they feel that they belong, and a community to which they attribute supreme

value. Such feelings of belonging makes life worth living. It also gives meaning and purpose to life in the family and the clan.

Many people, especially in Gesoni, still remember Sakagwa's last prophecy:

> "There are new people who are coming and they are not like us. They are like giant babies with the colour of new born babies. They will be wearing mushrooms on their heads and will be stronger than babies. They will be having metal sticks that will produce fire/smoke from them. The fire will not be like the one for cooking but will burn our houses down. Finally, these people will go back to their country. They will leave our country with more development and higher prosperity."

**SAKAWA D.E.B PRIMARY SCHOOL ADMINISTRATION BLOCK & CLASSROOMS
BACKGROUND: SAFARICOM & AIRTEL TOWERS**

SAKAWA D.E.B PRIMARY SCHOOL LOWER BLOCK

SAKAWA D.E.B PRIMARY SCHOOL UPPER PRIMARY BLOCK

THIS IS THE GESONI WATER PROJECT TANK. IT SUPPLIES WATER TO THE SCHOOL & THE COMMUNITY

PUPIL'S LATRINES

TEACHER'S LATRINES

THE GREEN VEGETATION & ROCKS THAT SURROUND THE "OMORAA TREE" AT GESONI HILL

THE WATER SPRING AT GESONI HILL WHERE THE PROPHET SAKAWA USED TO BATHE

Sakagwa's Legacy

Sakagwa played many roles in the Gusii society of his time, in the second half of the nineteenth century. He was medicine man, a war strategist, a community opinion leader, a prophet and more. He came to the scene when Abagusii were faced with existential threats, including persistent incursions from enemy tribes, famines occasioned by long droughts, animal diseases that could wipe entire livestock herds, and epidemics that threatened to wipe out the entire population. In addition, Abagusii lacked unity and common strategy for survival as a group. This society was greatly threatened.

All this required resilience, the role Sakagwa played in the survival of Omogisii cannot be denied. The frequent wars with the Maasai, Kipsigis and Luo needed an unerring strategist, consensus builder and foreteller of events if Abagusii were to survive.

Sakagwa, son of Ng'iti, was a product of his time and environment. As he grew up he saw the challenges and troubles Abagusii faced. He witnessed the split and persistent feuding along clan lines, and the harassment from all directions by their hostile and unrelated neighbours in Gusii society that knew no security.

Sakagwa, born in the clan of Bogeka, was brought up under the keen guidance of his father in a home that had strong spiritual grounding according to traditional beliefs. He progressively came face to face with the realization that the conventional behaviour (clanism and individualism) of the time was not a cementing factor of Abagusii society.

Under tutelage of his father he came to believe that *Engoro* and *chisokoro* sought him out to articulate their wishes to the erring people of Gusii; an intercessor for the people. Consequently, even in the face of opposition, and possible danger to his life, he laboured to point the way out of their problems.

What Abagusii specifically needed in the 19th Century was unity: unity to defend themselves against constant harassment and fatal attacks; and unity to act as a people in the interest of their social security and common destiny. In Ekegusii, there is a saying that *gakiaborire 'nchera maate kerigerie 'nchera rogoro* (if you cannot locate something you are looking for on one side of the path, try the alternative side). As such, if it was difficult to bring Abagusii together politically, then another way to do so was to appeal to them to cooperate first and to unite by invoking their common origin from their revered ancestors. This he combined with the use of spiritual beliefs of the time

Sakagwa knew that divided as they were, and surrounded on all sides by aggressive neighbours, Abagusii's very existence was threatened. But he also knew that should there be a major disaster, like pervasive famine, the already shrinking Gusii society could find it extremely difficult to ward off external aggression. It is no wonder that in the late 1880s he constantly warned the people against their petty differences and about inevitable impending doom if they did not change their ways. His warnings, whether by providence or coincidence, were proved right by the events of 1889 and 1890.

However, to Sakagwa, the occurrences of these events were less important than why they came. For him these problems were the direct judgement of *Engoro* and *chisokoro* on religious, political and social failure. We may go wrong if we think of him primarily as a legendary prophet of doom. However, Sakagwa represented more.

In his work, *Traditional History of the Gusii of Western Kenya,* Professor W. R. Ochieng', likens Sakagwa to the prophet Jeremiah of the Old Testament. Like Jeremiah, writes Ochieng', Sakagwa was concerned that Abagusii should mend their ways before it was too late. Even as Sakagwa was enunciating principles and norms that were critical during his time, he had an underlying message of reformation. And like Jeremiah, Sakagwa was patriotic and did not want his people to suffer God's wrath.

The view we have of Sakagwa (in terms of role, character and impact) is largely dictated by his activities which point to the personality of the seer himself. Clearly, this cannot be dissociated from the particular time in history during which he lived. And he was not just a prophet and all those other attributes that he demonstrated. All of this was conditioned by the fact that he lived through one of the most challenging times for Abagusii, when they could easily have been exterminated as a distinct people.

In going about his business (prophesying, treating illnesses, advising clan elders, strategizing for war, and many others) Sakagwa demonstrated love for the people. He was devastated to watch the impact of the raids from enemy ethnic groups and calamities such as famine, animal diseases and the like. Unlike the people (even prominent clan leaders) of his time, he was able to discern the mortal danger lurking in the horizon: the impending downfall of Abagusii society.

With the constant raids from the Maasai and the Kipsigis, the community was fast losing territory. According to Ochieng', by 1880 Abagusii hardly lived to the south of River Kuja. Because of the pressures from the Maasai and the Kipsigis, the territory occupied by Abagusii to the south of River Kuja is twice the area they occupied in 1880. Abagusii had lost most of their land to the Maasai (Trans Mara in Narok County) and the Kipsigis (areas in Bomet and Kericho counties).

Losing territory was one thing but Abagusii risked assimilation by the Luo and the Kuria. For example, as the Maasai and Kipsigis were pressing Abagusii, clans that bordered Luoland were fast undergoing acculturation, according to Ochieng'. At risk of this were the present-day Bogusero and Bonchari clans.

Sakagwa was right to be worried and his warnings may have been helped by the colonial rule that halted the trends. Colonialism made the ethnic boundaries more or less permanent and halted the persistent incursions of the raiding Maasai and Kipsigis.

*****

Given the danger the community faced, Sakagwa's message was predominantly of gloom and hopelessness. However, he also offered hope suggesting that unity could forestall the eventual doom that he predicted. In that respect, Sakagwa offered hope. And not only did he preach about what he foresaw but also worked consistently for the unity of Abagusii. It is this unity that earned victory for Abagusii at the battle of Osaosao. For once in a long time, perhaps a century, Abagusii had acted in unity.

Sakagwa's unity message and advice was not confined to the Gusii corporate level. He also advised individual clans on winning strategies, including North Mugirango where he spent a fair amount of his time and helped face Kipsigis warriors and South Mugirango where his actions enabled them to face the Maasai as a united group.

On South Mugirango, while advising against intra-clan divisions, he also offered practical strategies to win against the Maasai. In one instance he instructed them to bury alive a single-breasted girl and to face the Maasai as one single group. Upon heeding Sakagwa's instructions the people of Mugirango triumphed in the battle with the Maasai.

*****

Sakagwa's message was such that it initially brought him nothing but opposition, hatred and persecution. Only after the fulfillment of some of his prophecies (the famine of 1888 for example) did the power of his words move the minds of the people and persuade them that *chisokoro* had indeed been speaking to them through him. Over the years, he occupied a major perch as the spiritual leader of Abagusii.

It is no wonder that some of his ideas were still in force long after his death, and when Mumboism failed to provide a front for the dislodgement of the British, Abagusii turned to Sakagwaism, a name that had a special place in their hearts.

Once more, like Jeremiah of the Israelites, Sakagwa lived and died without the knowledge of Jesus Christ, and probably with no hope of a normal and happy future beyond the grave. He had no historical Jesus on whom to stake his life when doubt and despair assailed him. He only had the faith of his ancestors and the certainty that *Engoro*'s hand had been laid upon him so that he could save his people.

It is our view that Sakagwa's role, like that of many diviners and prophets in African societies, can be seen in terms of their attempts to explain circumstances and the implications of those circumstances on the plight of their societies. In solving societies' challenges, they actively attempted to shape and guide the destinies of those societies. For example, Sakagwa discerned that divisions among Abagusii weakened them in the face of attacks. He brought reason for unity among clans and such unity ensured Abagusii triumphed in the wars such as Osaosao.

*****

Further, we believe that individuals like Sakagwa also understood the spirituality of their communities, in addition to foretelling the future which was central to their roles. They understood their societies' view of the world, including the supernatural, and how this related to the individuals in that society as well and the society as a whole. For instance, Abagusii believed the existence of *chisokoro* and understood *chisokoro*'s intermediation role with the Supreme Being, *Engoro*. Sakagwa used this effectively in his trade including treating the sick and administering the oath of unity among clan leaders with respect to facing a common enemy. It can be inferred that Sakagwa, like other seers in many African societies, dispensed their advice and acted based on a reasonable chain of cause and effect. In the case of Abagusii, they needed to unite lest they be run over by enemy ethnic groups.

One can argue that such prophets' ability to communicate with the supernatural (*Engoro* via *chisokoro,* for example) enabled them to see with clarity the consequences (disaster or prosperity) of certain acts or conduct. But this is largely our evaluation of Sakagwa's life and character as a prophet.

In societies like Gusii of the time, all issues were intricately interwoven in a complex 'spider web' type, all-dimensional, mesh. Thus there was little distinction between the political and non-political. There was hardly a dividing line among such issues as politics, economics, medicine, spiritualty and other societal concerns. Life issues were intricately intertwined and any instructions given would be part of broad social action in the interest of the society.

It is in this respect that Sakagwa can be seen as a Gusii leader in the broad perspective. He used his complex abilities to acquire a central position in community leadership and respect. This leadership was spiritual, medicinal, political and otherwise. Above all, it was unelected and did not come by dint of clan leadership.

Note that the Gusii society of his time was fragmented. Leadership was decentralized with the clan as the highest unity of political organization and participation. His appeal for unity, and hence centralization of leadership, must have baffled many of his time, especially the clan leaders. Through persistent explanation of the flaws (military weakness and social decay) of the clan system, he was able to make the case for unity, lest the entire Abagusii face extinction.

In conducting these discussions, Sakagwa would chair most sessions where he constantly called on and persuaded participants to work together as one social and political team. This act elevated the sage to a level where he overshadowed even the strongest clan leaders who had their clan interest ahead of the welfare and security of the broader Gusii society.

Consequently, we can infer that Sakagwa saw himself as Omogusii first and Omogeka (a person from Bogeka clan) second. His constant communication was around Gusii wellbeing and was Gusii nationalism rather than parochial clan interests of the day. With this approach and acts, Sakagwa may have saved Gusii society from continued attrition and possible collapse.

Glossary of terms

Ekegusii	English Translation
Ababani; sing. *omobani*	Prophets/seers
Abanyamesira; sing. *omonyamesira*	Charm 'planters'
Abanyamete; sing. *omonyamete*	Medicine men
Abaragori; sing. *omoragori*	Fortune tellers
Abarogi; sing. *omorogi*	Witches/wizards
Abarumbasi	Arabs
Amandegere	A form of edible mushroom
Amandegere n'aame Getembe	Mushrooms will sprout at Getembe; Getembe was the original name of present-day Kisii Town
Chisokoro	Ancestors
Chinyangi; sing. *enyangi*	Rites of passage
Chindwaki; sing. *orwaki*	Forts
Chingoba sing. *engoba*	Woven animal skin that was won by women
Ebigendi bia Sakagwa	Small huts that Sakagwa built at Getembe, present-day location of Kisii Town
Ebiranya	A special magical concoction believed to have an effect on a subject to who it pertains especially in readiness for war

Glossary of Terms

Ebisarate; sing. *egesarate*	Encampments where young unmarried men stayed for purposes tutelage – character, defence technics, etc.
Ebisena sing. *egesena*	Pieces of woven skin won by the men around the groin area – front and back sides
Eburi	The original name g*esarate* which changed as the concept of *gesarate* evolved
Eero	The outer room of a traditional house in Gusii
Egesa	A hut in which the man of the home stayed
Egesangio	Group organized in such a manner that they help group members with work; once one called members to work (say) in tilling a *shamba* the person feed them and offered them alcohol, usually traditional brew
Egora	Veranda of a tradition house in Gusii
Ekamati	Sister of a woman's husband; wife of a woman's brother
Ekebure	A burial site (grave) inside the house
Ekerentane	An illegitimate child
Emeino	Special songs sung (usually by men) in drinking parties and the like
Emetembe	A plant that was common n Gusii and under which some rituals such as circumcision were carried out
Embori ya maikora	Goat of widowhood slaughtered to cleanse widow from spirits of her dead husband
Engoro	The name of God in Ekegusii

Enseka; plural *chinseka*	The largest of pots in Gusii used to hold water or traditional brew
Enyamakongiro	Famine that took place in the late 1800s that forced people to eat the Wandering Jew plant (*rikongiro*) that Abagusii do not typically consume as a vegetable
Enyamumbo	A movement is resistance against colonial rule that happened in the early 1900s
Esimbore	Ceremonial song for the initiate
Esegi y'Egetonto	The war of Osaosao
Esunyati	Ceremony and wedding apparel.
Etoto	Inner position wall in traditional house in Gusii
Gakiaborire 'nchera maate kerigerie 'nchera rogoro	A Gusii saying that suggests that if one option has failed, try another and (likely) opposite one
Gesarate	The place at *egesarate*
Getembe kia Gasuku	Getembe the place of Gasuku – Gasuku (Kasuku) was a court interpreter and people came to associate the place (Getembe – present-day Kisii Town) with Gasuku
Gosona i	Has a sensual connotation relating to admiring or to sensually provoke.
Irongo	An area (more like an attic) that was used for storage such things as food, pots, etc.
Irungu	Upper side of the place in inner room reserved for the wife of the home
Koria emuma	To swear an oath; to oath
Mobucha ibu	First wife

Glossary of Terms

Mosiereko	Door through partition inside a traditional house leading from inner room to the outer one *eero*
Ngoro ya Mwaga	A place (a cave) at the base of Manga Ridge where Abagusii used to conduct rituals and sacrifices.
Nyabweri maate	Fourth wife
Nyabweri rogoro	Third Wife
Nyageita	Fifth wife also known as *Nyagesieri* or *Nyamekorogoto*
Nyagesieri	Fifth wife also known as *Nyageita* or *Nyamekorogoto*
Nyakebee	Left-handed person
Nyamekorogoto	Fifth wife also known as *Nyageita* or *Nyagesieri*
Nyamesanchu	Second wife
Obokano	Traditional 8-stringed harp, a musical instrument
Obori	Finger millet
Olkoiyot	Term for seer in Kalenjin
Omobegu	A wrong-doer, a criminal
Omoboraka	Widower; a man whose wife has died and who has not married again
Omogomba	Childless woman
Omogoroka o'Sakagwa	A major cactus tree where Sakagwa held court in his homestead
Omoikora	Same as a *omoboraka*; a widower
Omoriakari	Newly-wedded or newly-married woman
Omotakanwa	A widow; woman whose husband has died and has not married again
Ongweso	A name that was given to Riogi's (son of Sakagwa) bull

Ong'ong'o	Rinderpest, a cattle disease
Orong'ang'a	A swam of locusts
Orwaki; plural. *chindwaki*	Fort
Ribina: plural. *amabina*	Rain dance usually directed by a rainmaker, and carried out largely by women, following a long dry spell
Rikongiro	Wandering Jew plant
Rioba nderera	'Sun' take care of my child

Bibliography

John S. Akama. *The Gusii of Kenya: Social, Economic, Cultural, Political & Judicial Perspectives.* Nsemia Inc. (February 2017).

John S. Akama. *The Untold Story of the Gusii of Kenya: Survival Techniques and Resistance to the Establishment of British Colonial Rule.* Nsemia Inc. (August 2019).

E. E. Barker. *The Short History of Nyanza.* East African Literature Bureau 1958.

Robert Levine. *Nyansiongo: a Gusii Community in Kenya.* Wiley.1956.

John Lowsdale. *The Conquest State 1895 – 1904.*

Enock B Matundura. *Kivuli Cha Sakagwa* (Swahili Edition) Nsemia Inc. (October, 2010).

Enock B Matundura (Author) with Kefa Otiso (Translator). *Sakagwa's Ghost.* Nsemia Inc. (November, 2020).

J. S. Mbiti *African Religious and Philosophy.* Heinemannn. 1969

R. M. Maxon. *The Gusii uprising of 1908* in *East Africa social council Conference Papers*, Kampala. 1969

Mayer, P. (1949). *The Lineage Principle in Gusii Society.* In Memorandum Oxford University Press. https://ehrafworldcultures.yale.edu/document?id=fl08-001

Mayer, P. (1950). *Gusii Bridewealth Law and Custom.* In Rhodes-Livingstone papers (Issue no. 18, pp. iv, 67).Oxford University Press. https://ehrafworldcultures.yale.edu/document?id=fl08-002

Evans Getuma Mogaka. *The Song of a Blacksmith and Totems of Abagusii.* 2019.

G. H. Mungeain. *The British Rule in Kenya, 1895 – 1912.* Oxford University Press. 1966.

King'oina Nyang'era. *The Making of Man and Woman under Abagusii Customary Laws.*

Roland Oliver and Gervase Mathew (Editors). *History of East Africa, Vol. 1.* Oxford University Press. 1961

H. Odera Oruka, *Sage Philosophy: The Basic Question,* in *Sage Philosophy: Indigenous Thinkers and Modern Debate on African Philosophy,* ed. H. Odera Oruka, E. J. Brill. 1990.

B. A. Ogot. A. *British Administration in the Central Nyanza District of Kenya, 1900-60.* In *The Journal of African History, vol. 4, no. 2, 1963, pp. 249–273.* JSTOR, www.jstor.org/stable/179537. Accessed 25 May 2021.

W. R. Ochieng' and B. A. Ogot. *Mumboism – An Anti-colonial Movement* in B. A. Ogot (editor) *War and Society in Africa.* 1972

W. R. Ochieng'. *A Pre-Colonial History of the Gusii of Western Kenya.* A.D. 1500 – 1914.

W. R. Ochieng' (editor). *A Modern History of Kenya 1895–1980: In Honour of Professor B. A. Ogot.* Nairobi: Evans Brothers, 1989.

W. R. Ochieng'. *A Traditional History of the Gusii of Western Kenya A.D. 1500-1914.* University of Nairobi Repository.

John N. B. Osogo. *Kenya's Peoples in the Past.* Longman. 1974.

Z. O. Ogamba. *Historical Reflection of Selected Women's Involvement in the Struggle for*

Kenya's Independence, 1920-1963. Masters' Thesis, Kenyatta University. 2017.

Jaspher Rori. *History and Culture of Abagusii.* Unpublished Manuscript 2010.

C. J. Wilson. *Before the dawn in Kenya: An authentic account of life in East Africa when it was under African rule.* English Press. 1952

Tryambe Zekeza. *The Establishment of Colonial Rule – 1905 – 1920.*